EMPATH

A Survival Guide for Highly Sensitive Person to Understand their Gift and Gain Self-Awareness. Learn how to Manage Anxiety, Stop Overthinking and Overcome Negative Emotions

William Cooper

professional before attempting any techniques outlined in this book.

By reading this document, the reader agrees that under no circumstances is the author responsible for any losses, direct or indirect, which are incurred as a result of the use of information contained within this document, including, but not limited to, — errors, omissions, or inaccuracies.

Table of Contents

Chapter 5
Empath's Sensitivities 83

Chapter 6
Empaths and Other People 95

Chapter 7
Developing Your Empath Skills 107

Chapter 8
Empath and Emotional Intelligence 119

Chapter 9
Empathy Ongoing: Your Tools at A Glance 135

Introduction

Congratulations on purchasing *Empath,* and thank you for doing so.

Empath is a term used for individuals with a preternatural insight into the emotional state of others. The following chapters will examine the nature of this gift, as well as the benefits and pitfalls that these individuals face. Being privy to the innermost feelings of others can be overwhelming, leaving those with said abilities to scramble for a way to combat the intense sensory overload.

It is our nature to fear what we do not understand. Having an ability beyond what is considered normal can leave those with gifts feeling othered and strange. Empaths often find their own emotional intensity to be cumbersome; they search for a means to suppress their abilities so that they might fit in. Misunderstanding sensitivity for weakness may lead some to distance themselves from their compassion.

There are tools that an empath can use to allow themselves to embrace their true nature while still managing to have control over their emotions. You should not feel that embracing your empathic tendencies will make you" too emotional" or weak in any way. In fact, once you learn to empower yourself, you will see that you are more gifted than you could have ever realized.

Having a clear understanding of how to overcome the challenges empaths face and how to tap into your power is one of the greatest gifts you can give yourself. We all deserve the right to be comfortable in our own skin, and the aim of this book is to help you manage your high sensitivity and develop your potential. Within these pages, you will learn to navigate the situations that used to strike fear into your heart.

There are plenty of books on this subject in the market, thanks again for choosing this one. Every effort was made to ensure it is full of as much useful information as possible, and please enjoy.

"It's this thing I have. I'm sorry if it scared you. I feel other people's feelings. I imagine crumbling insides and splitting hearts, goodbyes that hang in the air before they break into tiny pieces. I hear words that aren't said, the echoes of lonely hallways and hollow footsteps. I hear sobs that soak pillowcases when all the lights are out and the world is sleeping. I carry this inside of me, all of it."

— Jacqueline Simon Gunn

Chapter 1

Understanding the Empath

"You are too sensitive," "toughen up," "get a grip," or even "don't be a coward." These are common phrases that others often direct at those with empathic tendencies. Being overly sensitive is considered a sign of weakness. After all, we are meant to keep our emotions in check and remain reasonably in control of our feelings. Stoicism is celebrated in almost every culture, hailed as a mark of maturity.

Society teaches us to mask our feelings and present only those that are socially acceptable. Sure, it is okay to be distraught if your dog dies, but you can't really be that upset over the homeless guy sleeping under a bridge, or can you? Naturally, we all feel empathy when we see other people in pain. We sympathize when our friends are having a difficult time or when we see other people hurting. Most of us have built-in filters that allow us to separate other people's suffering from our own, in such a way that we can recognize it, we can sympathize with it, but we do not absorb it.

However, what if you felt everything around you as if it was happening to you? Imagine that you were unable to separate yourself from people's pain and experienced it yourself, both physically and emotionally. Watching the death of your favorite character on the silver screen would have prompted a reaction from you. You might have even cried uncontrollably as if you had lost a close friend.

Imagine that you were able to walk into a room and immediately pick up on the energy. You could read the emotional undercurrents beneath the surface of every smile. The feelings and experiences of others would overwhelm you as you absorb the sensations, like a sponge soaking up water. Hypersensitivity of this nature is the essence of being an empath.

What is an Empath?

Empaths are those with the innate ability to read and understand the emotions of people around them. This ability may even extend to nature, including plants and animals. Individuals with this sensitivity are able to read and absorb the energy of others, without even being aware that it's happening. This unconscious immersion means that the empathic party experiences feelings with the same depth and intensity as the person that held the sensations, originally.

Empaths have a higher level of natural intuition that stems from their ability to sense undercurrents of energy just below the surface. When interacting with another person, they can discern the mental and emotional state of that individual because they are hypersensitive to the world around them. Have you been in a situation where you had an intuitive feeling that something bad was going to happen? Empaths tend to see beyond the obvious, feeling before they think.

There is a charming stranger with a disarming smile. Average people will look at this individual in a superficial way, not reading beneath the surface. They are taken at face value; a smile means happiness. This is not the case for an empath, as they are able to detect negative energy that most of the population would miss. They would find themselves growing uneasy around this person whom everyone else is only able to see as normal.

People, by nature, are quite adept at concealing their feelings and thoughts. Others wear masks to hide evil intentions or negative emotions. That is why when someone commits suicide; it is common to hear friends and family state that the person seemed happy, and they did not see it coming. It takes more than sympathy to be able to go beyond putting yourself in the other person's shoes (empathy) to actually experiencing the emotions of the other person psychologically and physically.

An empath recognizes and feels the emotions that people will not talk about. Therefore, they have a much higher level of compassion and the ability to connect with others. There are no emotional defenses or barriers to shield them from absorbing the energy of the people they come into contact with and their surroundings. This makes individuals with this sensitivity more likely to be the "givers" in relationships.

A giver will not often say no, not because they do not want to, but because they cannot. They are likely to have people, the "takers', take advantage of their compassion. Empathy is a normal human trait. When we see others' in pain or in distress, we feel sympathy and may even want to help them. Empaths, however, experience the emotions of others on a much more intense scale than a normal person does.

The average person can feel sympathy and then walk away from a situation. Empaths cannot distance themselves in this way because they take in the emotion, and it becomes part of their own experience; they are not just spectating. These individuals absorb the suffering in others, making it their own.

Sinduthai Sapkal's Empath Experience

In a small village in India, a girl was born on a sweltering November day in 1948. Her parents would have rather had a boy since girls in their culture at the time, were nothing more than a burden and an extra mouth to feed. Still, Sinduthai was luckier than most in that she was spared the infanticide that was commonplace when unwanted daughters were born into a family.

Her father, to his credit, tried to send her to school, but fate intervened, and poverty put an end to her formal education after the fourth grade. With no use for her, she was married off at the tender age of nine to a man who, in his thirties, was more than two decades her senior. Knowing no other way of life, Sinduthai, at nine, became a wife and a mother of three by the time she was twenty years old.

Fate, however, was not done with Sinduthai, and after some village chatter, her husband was incited into getting rid of his wife, who at the time happened to be pregnant. She was battered by her husband and left for dead in the cow pen, where the cows were expected to trample on her and, in so doing, provide a plausible explanation of her death. It is in this cow-pen that a barely alive Sinduthai gave birth to her daughter and managed to escape to a nearby cemetery that she called home for a while with nowhere else to go.

Begging on the streets to feed herself and her daughter, Sinduthai was confronted by the sheer numbers of children abandoned and left to die in the streets with no one to care for them. She resolved to make them her responsibility. So, she begs for herself, her daughter, and the abandoned children. She adopted these children of the streets, even though she could barely feed herself or her daughter, and had nothing but love to offer them.

Eventually, after years of begging, a Good Samaritan took notice of the woman herding and taking care of numerous street children. This savior built an orphanage so that Sinduthai and her adopted children would have a place to call home. With time, Sinduthai found donors to fund the education of her adopted children, and she managed to raise and nurture over a thousand street children.

However, for this remarkable woman, her journey was not quite over. The same husband who left her for dead showed up on her doorstep in tatters and homeless. Unsurprisingly for her, Sinduthai took him in and offered him the grace and compassion he was never able to give to her or her daughter.

Sinduthai Sapkal is now a renowned social activist, and is fondly referred to as the "mother of orphans." She has won numerous local and international awards for her charity work. It baffles many, that a woman, who had nothing, could be so compassionate towards others. They wonder how she found the strength to not only save herself but for many others who, like her, had been discarded and abandoned. Sinduthai is the embodiment of an empath who cannot help but feel other people's pain and is helpless in the face of people's distress and suffering, to the point of forgetting her own needs and only thinking of others.

We may not all be driven to great acts of charity or life-changing paths by a compassionate nature, however, as an empath, you will always be unable to distance yourself or ignore the pain of others. An empath is highly sensitive to other people's needs, and in either small or big ways, they make an impact on humanity since they are drawn to the service of others and are compelled to cater to the needs of people in the throes of misfortune.

Scientific Explanations of Empathy and Empaths

Research has shown that there are scientific factors that predispose people to become empaths. These factors affect how emotions are processed and how we react to the environment and the people around us. Some of these biological factors include;

The Mirror Neuron System

The mirror neuron system is a group of specialized brain cells that are responsible for our ability to mimic other people's actions and behavior. These specialized brain cells enable us to feel other people's pain, joy, happiness, or any other emotions. In empaths, this mirror neuron system is more sensitive than in the average person. This means that once stimulated by external factors, this system triggers a much stronger psychological reaction.

The mirror neuron system is triggered by our surroundings and the external environment, ever noticed how you tend to be happier when you are surrounded by positive and upbeat people? This happens because we take on the emotions of those around us. If you surround yourself with negative people, you tend to feel more negative yourself. This is beyond a social phenomenon. These specialized brain cells responsible for mirroring other people will pick up on the mood of those around you, and soon, it becomes your energy. "The misery loves company" may be a cliché, but science has proven that we tend to model ourselves after our environment and the emotions of the people in it.

While empaths have a highly active mirror neuron system that increases their sensitivity to other people, the opposite happens in psychopaths and narcissists. The same system in individuals with the aforementioned personality disorders is almost nonfunctional, and this explains why these two groups of people can inflict pain without feeling compassion or sympathy. When the mirror neuron system is weak, we can only feel our own emotions, and thus, it becomes difficult to be compassionate, understanding, or kind to people.

Electromagnetic Fields

The brain and heart produce electromagnetic fields as a form of energetic communication. Typically, information about an individual's emotions and mental state is encoded in these electromagnetic fields that are generated by the heart and brain. Research carried out on a person experiencing two distinct and opposite emotions (appreciation and anger) showed a clear distinction between the electromagnetic fields produced during the two emotional states.

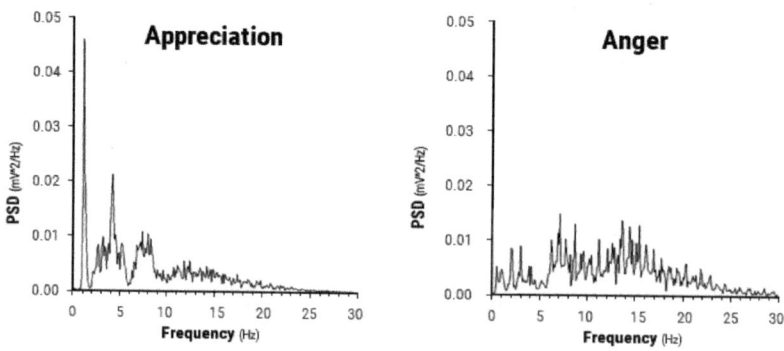

Communication between two people occurs on various levels apart from the obvious verbal interaction. There is an electromagnetic exchange that occurs below the conscious level, contributing to the scale of emotional connection that we are able to establish with the other person.

Empaths are highly in tune with this subconscious communication, which is why they can discern emotions even when they are not immediately visible or verbally articulated. This higher level of sensitivity to electromagnetic communication has also been credited for the gifts of nature empaths and their ability to read the energy of plants and animals.

Emotional Contagion

When the thoughts and behavior of an individual precipitate others feeling and acting in the same way, this phenomenon is referred to as emotional contagion. This influence can be affected through conscious or subconscious triggers, meaning that even when we are not aware of it, we can be deeply altered through other people's experiences. This is especially true for empaths who naturally have a high sensitivity to other people's emotional states.

Emotional contagion has been found to exist in personal relationships, as well as professional situations where people are required to work in teams. On a personal level, it is common to find that even a young child can pick up on feelings of distress in their mother, and these emotions can also cause the child to become troubled. The youth are highly intuitive; they are ruled by senses rather than cognitive aptitude and, as such, can pick up on emotional signals that we think are beyond their understanding.

In group situations, the mood of one person (either positive or negative) has the ability to affect the whole team. The atmosphere changes based upon the energy being projected by any given person. Such emotional contagion can be overwhelming for intensely empathetic people. An overload of sensory stimuli and feelings from so many different sources can be exhausting and may even act as a social deterrent. The intimidating nature of these interactions is enough to send empaths running. Scientific studies suggest that these individuals are more likely to be introverted than extroverted, favoring limited social contact.

Increased Dopamine Sensitivity

Dopamine is a chemical that is released by nerve cells in the brain to transmit messages to other cells. It, therefore, functions as a neurotransmitter. This substance is regarded as a "feel-good hormone" and is responsible for mood elevation and a positive emotional state when released in the body.

Empaths have been found to have a higher sensitivity to dopamine. Even trace amounts, when released into the body, may have a dramatic effect on mood. This increased susceptibility to such hormones may explain why these individuals are affected, to a larger degree, by emotions when compared to the average person.

Synesthesia

Synesthesia is a neurological factor that connects two senses that are normally not linked. For instance, a person with synesthesia can smell a particular scent when listening to a song or associate a noise with a certain color. In these cases, two senses are used to interpret external stimuli that would typically be perceived using only one.

Ordinarily, when you hear a song, you do not associate it with a scent or color because it is only processed in the brain as sound. Synesthetes perceive reality in a different way. They are able to make associations between unrelated senses, such as sight (hue) and smell.

In empaths, mirror-touch synesthesia enables them to feel the emotional and mental state of the other person as if it is happening in them as well.

Characteristics of an Empath

Neurological differences, like the ones discussed above, can predispose some to an empathic nature. Superficially visible markers may also separate these individuals from the rest of the population. Some of these characteristics include:

Empaths Are Highly Intuitive

Most people have a gut instinct that enables them to sense certain feelings in others. For example, mothers are highly intuitive when it comes to their children. Some can tell when their baby is unwell even before physical symptoms of any illness present. The deep emotional connection they have with their little one enables them to discern things that others cannot.

In empaths, these hunches are highly developed due to their sensitivity. They can easily read people and situations using their intuition. The average person, while they may have these telling gut feelings, will not pay them much mind because most people tend to logic-driven. However, these highly perceptive individuals will trust their emotions more, and this explains why empaths develop a keen sixth sense since they rely on it to read situations and people in their environment.

Empaths Are Highly Sensitive

We always laugh at that one friend who cries in movies or when they hear a certain song. It can be hard to understand why a person would be profoundly affected by a fictional story or performance. However, for empaths, the lack of mental barriers to separate themselves from external emotions means that they feel situations as if they are happening to them and not as spectators.

Empaths typically have a low threshold for stimulation, meaning that they are easily triggered by external stimuli and affected by outside forces. This high sensitivity means that they have a difficult time distinguishing pain felt by others from their own. Those with empathic tendencies will experience suffering just as deeply as the person who originated the feeling.

The spectrum for sensitivity is illustrated below:

Narcissists	Average people	Highly Sensitive people	Empaths
I	I	I	I
Lowest sensitivity			Highest sensitivity

Empaths Are Selfless

Empaths will give others the shirt off their back, literally. Empaths are kind and incapable of letting other people suffer. They have a high level of compassion. These individuals will do anything to make others feel better, even at their own expense. While most of us do have sympathy and are willing to assist others as much as we can, we retain a level of self-interest that enables us to safeguard our needs even while we are engaged in acts of charity.

An average person called upon for aid will give what they are comfortably able to miss. Self-preservation encourages a prioritizing of the self over others. When the needs of others exceed the ordinary person's capability to help, the assistance will cease.

Empaths behave in stark contrast to this norm; there is no end or limit to how far they will go to help others. Their compassion is so immense that they are often taken advantage of. Narcissists are especially dangerous to sensitive individuals, for these reasons.

Empaths Connect Easily with Others

Empaths are good at reading and internalizing other people's feelings. This means that for them, forming an emotional connection comes naturally. The average person will take time to get to know a person's attributes and values before opening up to them.

Individuals with compassionate tendencies are able to form these bonds quickly. It is not uncommon to see an empath creating an intense personal bond to someone that they have just met. There are no walls or filters slowing the advancement of these interpersonal relationships.

This trait can make others shy away from them because the deep connection established in a very short time seems unnatural to those who are not empaths. The average person will take time to establish a deep emotional bond. Meeting someone who behaves outside of the norm in such a forward way can be frightening to some.

Empaths Are Introverted

In most cases, empaths will be introverts. Due to their high sensitivity to other people's feelings and external stimuli, they develop a natural tendency to limit social interactions to avoid sensory overload. They are content in their own company and do not need constant communication with others to be happy. Groups boasting large numbers can be overwhelming for these individuals, as they are always receiving this emotional data. Avoiding crowds and populated activities is just a more reasonable option.

Empaths Are Easily Distracted

Empaths are absent-minded by nature and are easily distracted. These individuals are able to sense energy and emotions running just beneath the surface. This constant intake of information can result in a loss of focus. Empaths are easily sidetracked by their own intuition. They tend to notice all the bright and shiny things, as well as the dark ones that the average person would miss while immersed in their actual tasks. They also have a tendency to daydream, becoming lost in a world of their own creation. All of these factors compound to paint sensitive people in a way that seems out-of-touch with the present.

Highly Creative

Empaths are very emotionally driven and intuitive, which enhances their imagination. They have a natural affinity for arts such as music, writing, painting, and other creative pursuits. They excel better in fields that require higher emotional awareness than fields that are more dependent on cognitive aptitudes such as accounting or law.

Free-Spirited

Most empaths find rules and tight restrictions to be confining and limiting. They are often free-spirited and deplore routines and structured environments. These individuals value freedom of expression, thought, and action. Independence and originality are very important.

Nature Lovers

Empaths love spending time outside. They enjoy communing with nature and are rejuvenated by the life that surrounds them. Empathic individuals are content to spend their days in the company of mother earth, taking long walks through thick forests or lounging on scenic beaches. Some are even able to extend their compassionate connections out to the flora and fauna that they so admire, drinking up the energy that reverberates through the world around them.

Are You an Empath?

Are you an empath? By taking an honest look at your own thoughts and actions, you will be able to determine if you meet the requirements. It is important to remember that most people are not devoid of compassion. Empaths are an extreme on the altruistic spectrum of human behavior characterized by their sensitivity to the emotions of others and their ability to absorb the feelings and experiences of those around them.

The following questions will enable you to determine if you are an empath:

- Am I frequently described as overly sensitive?

- Do I have a tendency to get overwhelmed or uncomfortable, especially in groups and large social gatherings?

- Do I constantly feel like the odd one out or find it hard to fit in?

- Do I find crowds exhausting and emotionally draining?

- Do I often need time alone to collect my thoughts and calm myself?

- Am I averse to excessive external stimulation such as noisy environments or odors?

- Am I put off or overwhelmed by incessant chatter and people who talk too much?

- Do I often prefer to take my own car to places so that I can leave early if I need to?

- Do I find myself developing a stress-coping mechanism to mitigate the damage from emotional overloads, such as overeating or drinking alcohol?

- Do I feel like I tend to lose my identity in intimate relationships?

- Am I easily alarmed?

- Do I have a strong reaction to medication or caffeine?

- Do I have a tendency to avoid confrontation and arguments?

- Do I have a low threshold for pain?

- Am I likely to prefer alone time and tend to socially isolate?

- Do I find myself absorbing other people's emotions, distress, or even physical symptoms?

- Am I easily distracted?

- Do I prefer freedom and independence and hate structured and controlled environments?

- Do I find nature rejuvenating?

- Does it take me a long time to relax after a long day or after interacting with people?

- Do I feel better in quiet environments such as the countryside than I do in bustling environments such as cities?

- Do I find one-on-one interactions better than group interactions?

Once you have answered the above questions, you can then interpret the results using the following guide;

- ✓ 1 – 5 yes answers = partial empath tendencies.

- ✓ 6 –10 yes answers = moderate empath tendencies.

- ✓ 11- 15 yes answers = strong empath tendencies.

- ✓ 15 plus yes answers = full-blown empath.

Chapter 2

The Different Types of Empaths

Psychopaths aside, a large proportion of humanity is capable of empathy, which is the ability to put ourselves in someone else's shoes. Compassion allows us a basic understanding of the needs and emotions of others. The feelings that allow us to relate to those around us are the groundwork for humanity's inherent altruism. These traits are biologically necessary for the furthering of our species so that we are encouraged to act as a community.

Empathy can be in many different forms, including:

Cognitive empathy – this kind of empathy is concerned with being able to understand someone else's views or perspectives. It does not have much to do with compassion but rather the recognition that other people have different beliefs and perceive the world in their own way, their own thoughts and experiences have influenced a worldview that looks nothing like your own.

For instance, if you work with other people, you know that it is not possible to always have the same opinion on issues, as your colleagues. Cognitive empathy is the skill that enables you, in such situations, to understand the other person's point of view and where they are coming from. Cognitive empathy is, therefore, a vital skill for negotiation as well as establishing functional relationships where people with divergent views have to come together.

People who don't have cognitive empathy will find it difficult to work well with others; it speaks to narrow mindedness. Imagine the absurdity associated with expecting others to have had the same experiences as you, leading them to the same opinions. We are all a product of our genetics and our environment, a mixture that is completely unique to every individual. It is imperative to be able to relate to stories that are not our own in order to achieve success in any given situation.

Emotional empathy – Emotional empathy is true to its name. *Cognitive* is a reference to mental abilities and our perception. *Emotional* is a deep and primal word that wants to know what we are feeling. The core of human existence is made up of these feelings; they are tangled up in our decisions, psychological state and the caliber of relationships that we forge with one another.

Emotional empathy wants you to understand the sorrow, joy, rage, and fear of others. These and other feelings inform the actions of every human, they are the fuse to our behavior. A mother can identify when her child is unhappy because she has a deep connection with the child; she knows what suffering looks like and is aware of her own experience with sadness. She can draw upon her own knowledge to relate to the crying of her newborn. These relays occur so quickly that we are often unaware. We see a friend in trouble and know that something is wrong with only a glance. Our emotions are a big part of who we are, and whether consciously or subconsciously, we wear them wherever we go. Truly empathic people can read these clues faster and with more intensity than we could ever dream.

Emotional empathy enables you to understand other people's thoughts and feelings. This skill is, therefore, important in establishing good personal relationships, enabling a deep connection between parties. This ability is also important in service-oriented professions where you need to interact with and reassure people, such as doctors or nurses who need to provide comfort.

Compassionate empathy – this type of empathy can be described as *active empathy*. This is the trigger that moves you to act after recognizing the emotions and perspectives of others. Compassion goes beyond crying with your friend when they are in distress. Motivating sympathy moves you to alleviate their pain by helping them solve the problem.

Compassionate empathy is the driving force behind philanthropists and activists who devote themselves to helping people and alleviating the suffering of others. It goes beyond *cognitive empathy* and *emotional empathy* and inspires action to improve the lives of other people. Change occurs when people are motivated to reach out and help those who are less fortunate.

It is possible for a person to exhibit all, a couple or just one of the different types of empathy. Compassionate empathy is a complex creature that is built upon the backs of the other two forms, so they must be present (one or both) for an individual to present this type. People are complicated and all of us are different. The ways that we think and feel are specific to us. There are so many labels that are meant to categorize our behavior, from the way that we think to the type of sympathy that we feel. The most important sentiment is that humans are able to recognize our own experiences within others and we use this relation to inform our actions.

The common ground in all the three different types of empathy is that an empath is able to think, feel, and act beyond their self-interests. It is impossible to behave in this manner if you have no understanding of other people's emotions and views. This means that social awareness is a crucial element for empathic individuals. If you are perpetually focused on your own feelings, needs, and perspectives, there is no room left to develop compassion and understanding of others.

This is most evident in narcissists, who are incapable of thinking or feeling beyond their own needs. These individuals lack empathy and understanding for others and often view people as a means to an end. They require attention (negative and positive) and beyond that, they have no objection. Narcissists are the antithesis of empaths, which absorb the emotions of others and may forget their own needs in the process of caring about the people around them.

Empaths may have stronger attributes in one area than others. These distinctions manifest in differing labels, found through observing the areas of strength. Empathic individuals may be labeled as one of the following:

- Emotional Empath
- Physical/Medical Empath
- Geomantic Empath
- Claircognizant/Intuitive Empath
- Animal Empath
- Plant Empath

Emotional Empath

Have you ever put on a façade to disguise your emotions? Think of being in the company of someone you do not like, but you have to be polite and friendly. Or even a bad date you had to sit through. It is an excruciating and boring time, but you feel obligated to maintain the appearance of happiness. We all, at one time or another, have had to mask our emotions, either to protect ourselves or others.

An emotional empath is able to decipher even what lies beneath the surface. This is because their ability to sense such energy does not occur on a cognitive level but rather, subconsciously. Emotional empaths can pick up on the general feelings and small nonverbal cues that display our true emotions. In fact, not only do they recognize the innermost thoughts of others, they absorb these sensations and feel them in their own bodies.

This innate ability to pick up on and internalize feelings from external sources means that emotional empaths can and do establish deep connections with people within a very short time. In normal circumstances, the average person will take much longer to develop an interpersonal connection with others because it takes time to get to know the other party and understand their essence. People are not usually simple; they aren't easy reads. In contrast, the emotional empath is able to form a more substantial bond with haste. This is because they are able to confidently comprehend others in a way that encourages that intimate attachment.

For emotional empaths, being in crowds and groups can be overwhelming and exhausting. In these situations, they absorb feelings and sensations from multiple sources, and this becomes overstimulating for their hypersensitive nature. This is why you will find that emotional empaths are more comfortable in individual interactions as opposed to situations that involve large numbers of participants.

For an emotional empath, it is difficult to separate the feelings of other people from their own. They lack the filters that average people use to safeguard themselves from getting too involved with other people's affairs. In fact, emotional empaths tend to get lost in intimate relationships because they absorb all the wants, needs and tastes of their partner and lose elements of themselves in the process.

Emotional empaths who have not yet cultivated their ability to protect their own energy and boundaries may find themselves prone to mood swings, unexplained anger, or depression. This is because they may not be consciously aware that they are absorbing the energy of the people around them. It can feel a bit like they are going crazy. A plethora of new and unexpected thoughts and feelings wash over these empaths, like a tidal wave. The sensation of drowning in the unknown is enough to overwhelm anyone.

Physical/Medical Empath

Physical empaths have the ability to pick up on the energy from other people's bodies. This means they are highly sensitive to other people's physical pain or ailments. In some cases, they can actually feel the soreness of the other person in their own bodies. The ability of physical empaths to intuitively know where the other person's ache or illness is in their body means that they make great healers both in conventional medicine and alternative medicine.

When a physical empath is in the room with someone with a migraine, they might start experiencing a headache as well. Similarly, if they are engaging with someone who is fatigued or stressed, they will feel their energy levels start to lag and mirror those of the other person. This is what makes them great healers because they can sense what the other individual is ailing from without being told.

Physical empaths are highly intuitive and will pick up on signs and symptoms that other people may not see, including the person experiencing them. This type of empath is also prone to picking up empathic illnesses from other people. These individuals can, therefore, suffer from unexplained ailments and may even be considered hypochondriacs.

A physical empath needs to develop a mechanism to protect from picking up ailments and pains from other people. This requires them to avoid toxic energy that may affect them physically. To determine whether or not you are a physical empath, you can self-diagnose by asking.

- Do I feel other people's physical pain or even anxiety in my body?

- Do I feel perpetually tired or suffer from many unexplained ailments?

- Have I been described as a hypochondriac or taken medical tests that show no signs of illness despite feeling sick?

- Do crowds make me feel tired, exhausted, or stressed for no apparent reason?

If most of these traits are true for you, then you may be a physical empath.

Geomantic Empath

Geomantic empaths develop deep connections with particular geographical locations. They are also known as environmental empaths; they feel a presence or certain energy that draws them to any given place. When they leave their ideal atmosphere, they feel uncomfortable and find it hard to relax or adjust to other habitats or scenery.

Most geomantic empaths are drawn to ancient places where things may have happened in the past, such as old churches, ruins, or even cemeteries. They feel the undercurrents in their environment and sense the energy that their surroundings are giving off. This kind of sensitivity can turn a person very drawn to a particular place or destination and very averse to others depending on the vibe they pick up from the place.

If you find yourself feeling inexplicably happy, at ease or rejuvenated while in a particular location, this could be a sign that you are a geomantic empath. This is especially true if you also find yourself repelled by other environments, with your body reacting negatively to the change in scenery. Pay attention to your comfort levels the next time that you are on the road. That shiver could mean more than you initially give it credit for.

Claircognizant/Intuitive Empath

The claircognizant empath is highly intuitive and has the ability to see and sense things beyond the surface. They combine clear seeing (clairvoyance) and clear hearing (clairaudience) abilities to achieve claircognizance or the clear knowing ability. These individuals rely on their natural gut instincts to predict what is likely to happen. They are also very good at seeing people's real intentions and identifying fake or dishonest people.

The claircognizant empath is sensitive to other people's energy and can decode it quickly. Sometimes their abilities can border on the telepathic in their ease of reading other people's thoughts, emotions, and intentions. They are a preternatural judge of character. An intuitive empath will develop a sense of the person they are meeting with as soon as they first come in contact with them and are, therefore, good at identifying potentially dangerous or harmful situations. This kind of empath will warn a friend or colleague to stay away from a particular individual even when the other person is not able to see anything wrong with the person they are being warned about.

Claircognizant empaths are also highly imaginative and creative. They are good at coming up with innovative ideas on the spur of the moment. Some other common characteristics in intuitive empaths are:

- They can easily see read people and identify a fake person from a trustworthy one.

- They have an innate sixth sense that tells them if something is wrong.

- They can predict things that will happen in the future.

- They have an uncanny ability to find lost objects and items.

- They are excellent problem solvers.

- They are very creative and make great songwriters and authors.

Animal Empath

We have all heard of, or seen television shows featuring, horse or dog whisperers. These individuals seem to possess an otherworldly link to the fauna around them. Animal empaths have emotional connections to both pets and wildlife; they are able to decode and understand the innermost feelings of their subjects. Individuals with this sensitivity may also display a preference for a specific species, finding that their abilities work the best when directed at cats, fish, etc. These empaths feel the most at peace when they are in the company of other creatures.

Animal empaths are usually distressed by situations where animals are kept in captivity or mistreated. They tend to gravitate to professional fields that focus on the care and wellbeing of animals. These individuals are likely to be vegetarian.

Plant Empath

A plant empath has a natural affinity for greenery. They are at their best when surrounded by trees and vegetation. They are considered to have a green thumb, meaning that they are good at taking care of and nurturing flora. They know intuitively where to place flowers, how much sunlight they need, or how often they should be watered. Plant empaths may feel that they can channel the energy from trees and may feel rejuvenated when surrounded by vegetation.

Despite their strengths being in various areas, empaths share a common deep need to understand and connect with their environment, whether it is in the form of other people, animals, plants, or other forms of nature. In all, their sensitivity to external emotions is high, and this is what gives them the ability to connect with different aspects of their environment. Empaths are givers, feeling their best when able to connect to their element.

Empaths effortlessly draw things to them. They inspire a sense of trust that makes people feel comfortable around them; even animals feel this draw, which is why you will find that most are pretty good at handling and taking care of animals. Simply put, they are the healers in our midst. They're the nurturers who mother, protect and sustain. These individuals are the sensitive lovers that give and give with no reservations. Though considered rare, 15-20% of the population is actually made up of empaths.

Chapter 3

Accepting the Gift of Empath

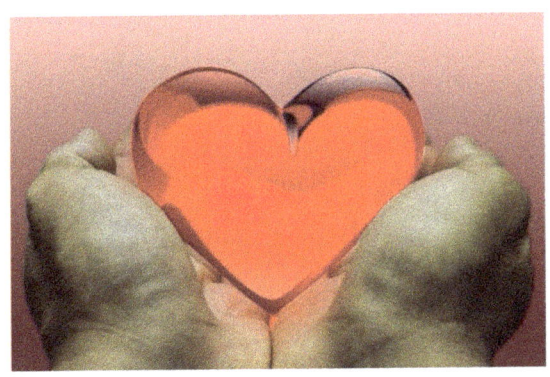

Empath, Intuition and Extraordinary Perceptions

Fitting in, being 'normal,' and conforming may sound trite, but to tell the truth, most people spend their lives trying to do just that. From childhood, our differences make us outsiders and we try to cover them up so that we do not get a 'weird' brand or, worse still, get bully for it. It doesn't stop as we get older because when you do not assimilate to the standard set by society, you become a misfit or a loner.

For empaths, this is a struggle that they have to learn to deal with because, for most people, their heightened sensitivity makes them too "emotional" or "weak." It is hard for people to understand why your moods shift suddenly, for no apparent reason; why you won't enter a particular place when you have a 'bad feeling.' So, they develop coping mechanisms early in life to help them overcome, if not disguise their highly sensitive natures.

Some of the coping mechanisms that empaths use are;

1. Shape-shifting

Even from a young age, empaths are easily able to tell what people want through their ability to read their emotions. When trying to fit in, in most cases, they try to be what others want them to be. Empaths learn to hide their sensitivities by acting tough or putting on a defensive or rebellious exterior. This is especially true for children who grow up hearing, "stop being a sissy," "toughen up," or similar phrases.

In groups, empaths tend to mirror the actions of others to fit in. They can adapt the appropriate appearance, demeanor, and behavior to be seen to conform to the norm or acceptable standards. The drive to change from who they really are, to the person that others wish them to be, comes from the empathic impulse to people-please. Individuals with these tendencies want nothing more than to make others happy. Sometimes bending to the whim of parents, friends, and teachers is a means to fulfill this goal. This can be especially true if the other party mandates a change from them.

In an intimate relationship, an empath can change their appearance, manner of dressing, or any other aspect of their personality to please their partner. This leaves them susceptible to undue influence from manipulative and narcissistic people. These individuals are the sociopath's dream.

2. Suppressing emotions

For most empaths, emotions can be overwhelming. Since they absorb feelings from the people around them, they are prone to unexplained mood swings and feeling drained by other people's stressors. This hypersensitivity to external stimuli makes these individuals prone to what the average person would call an "overreaction." It is hard for other people to understand why seemingly small things affect the empath so much or so deeply. Therefore, to avoid being perceived as "oversensitive," most learn to suppress their impulses as a coping mechanism.

An empath, by nature, feels before they can think; their intuition drives their world. When dealing with others, they need to appear as "not too much." They are hesitant to share their emotions. This leads to situations where they may prefer spending time alone to process their own emotions. In fact, research has shown that most empaths tend to be introverts.

Imagine a scenario in which an empath is in an intimate

relationship and feels unfulfilled or unappreciated by their partner. They will not voice their feelings or concerns and are most likely to go along with the situation even if they are unhappy. This is because they are afraid of being labeled "needy" or "clingy." Suppressing emotions is a common coping mechanism used by empaths in their relationships, whether on a personal, romantic, or professional level.

3. Turn off or tune out

What do empaths do when they are overwhelmed by emotions? If you are constantly soaking up emotions from your environment sooner or later, they are bound to overwhelm you. In this case, the empath looks for easy ways to turn down or turn off the sentimental overload. While there are healthy ways to do this, there are also many bad habits that these individuals develop as a coping mechanism to get away from their feelings.

Activities like overeating, alcohol consumption, or even drug use provide a temporary escape for empaths who do want to get away from their emotions. These activities work because they are effective in distracting any person from the present. Even for an average individual, feeling sadness or anxiety can cause them to seek solace in food, addiction, or compulsive shopping. The weight of emotions on an empathic mind is much higher. Therefore, they are more likely to resort to such coping mechanisms as a means of escaping the constant onslaught of changing feelings and moods.

A tuning out, for an empath, can also mean limiting social interactions or avoiding them altogether. You will find that most tend to shy away from large groups and prefer one on one interactions or solitude. This ultimately is just a means to minimize emotional input because having to deal with too many sensations all at once is not only draining; it can cause physical fatigue as well.

Jake's Empath Experience

Growing up, I found myself constantly feeling ill and uncomfortable in crowds or groups. I could not explain, even to myself, why I was so anxious and stressed out in group situations. Naturally, I began to avoid large groups and would always hide away when we had relatives over or when we visited other people. It just felt safer and more comfortable to be in my own company.

I felt everything around me, and it was all too much, so I found a way to deal with it by staying out of situations where I would be in the company of people. Even in school, I preferred playing games in solitude. It's not that I was unfriendly or even reserved; it just felt like the more people I was around, the more people I would have to take care of and appease. The classroom felt like a prison of sorts because I could not escape the constant pressure from everyone's conflicting emotions and needs. Away from school, I had a hard time getting to sleep or eating well because, at the same time, I would be thinking of the homeless guy I saw on the way home and wondering where he was sleeping or if he had anything to eat. This sense of helplessness and the unfairness of the world was overwhelming.

Of course, my parents worried about me and my seemingly unexplained anxieties and inability to fit in or make friends. They suspected I was suffering from an anxiety or attention-deficit disorder. Eventually, they took me to a therapist. This was the turning point in my life. I discovered I was not a "weirdo" or a "sap' as the bullies called me; in fact, I learned there was nothing wrong with me.

I discovered instead that I am an ultrasensitive empath. My therapist blesses her, recognized what was going and shared her own experiences in coming to terms with her own empathic nature. From that moment, even though I was only 13, I felt free and able to embrace who I was. I learned through her that it was Ok to be sensitive and that I did not have to camouflage or suppress my feelings. She taught me to embrace the gift of being an empath.

The Gift of Being an Empath

Heightened awareness and sensitivity to other people's emotions may sometimes overwhelm you and feel like a burden. The constant emotional overload may drive some to use the coping mechanisms we have discussed earlier in the chapter. However, when you start embracing your true nature, the sensitivities, intuition, and other empathic traits and gifts that you can use to improve not just your own life but also the lives of other people.

Some of the gifts of being an empath are;

- **Empaths are natural healers**

  Your innate ability to detect and understand other people's pain makes you a natural healer and nurturer. You can easily bring comfort to those in pain because you understand and feel their plight. Your natural compassion makes you want to alleviate suffering, so without even trying, an empath is a natural healer. People can feel better just from being around you.

- **The gift of intuition**

  Your intuitive nature and powerful sixth sense serve as a compass that guides you toward good and directs you away from the bad. The ability to see beyond the obvious is one of the empath's most powerful gifts. It's like having a direct channel to your inner wisdom that gives you better clarity and understanding of situations.

  How many times has your intuition led you to be at just the right place in just the right moment? How many times have you avoided a disaster by taking a different route or choosing a different path? What may appear as lucky coincidence may actually be your intuition acting as an inner compass.

- **Deep connections**

  People you have just met feel like they have known you for years. You are easy to connect to because you understand others so deeply. This makes it easier for people to bond with you. You make friends for life, and your ability to perceive other people's emotions and know what they need makes you one of the best friends a person can have. Empaths do not have superficial relationships; they are all characterized by deep emotional connections.

- **Simplicity**

You have a deep appreciation for the simple things in life. Nature, peace, and quiet or just time alone are enough to keep you happy and rejuvenated. You have the capacity to feel every moment and channel positive energy. For you, emotions rule your heart, and love and being loved are your ultimate goals. This means that you will not be bogged down chasing material possessions or status; your happiness comes from making other people happy.

- **Compassion**

The world needs more compassion, and you, the empath, have this in abundance. There are always people in need or in pain. We can touch their lives in small ways or big ways by simple acts of kindness. Simply spending time with an elderly person, feeding someone who is hungry, or volunteering at a children's hospital can make a significant difference in someone else's life. Fortunately for you, acts of altruism come naturally. You are your happiest when giving to others. There can never be too much benevolence in the world, and empaths help to make the world a much better place for the people they help.

- **Emotional Contagion.**

An empath is very good at spotting bad influences and toxic energy. This means they are able to surround themselves with positive people who channel only good energy. The net result of this is that empaths tend to be happy by surrounding themselves with things and people that make them thus. Goodness is contagious, and as empaths, we tend to take on the emotions and energy of the people we let into our circle.

- **Creative and innovative**

Empaths use their feelings to project their artistic and creative talents. This means that they can express their feelings in a way other people cannot. They tend to be gifted in arts such as music, painting, and even writing because of their emotionally driven nature. These individuals feel before they think and, therefore, see things in a unique and special way. As an empath, you are good at coming up with new ideas and have a different perspective on issues. You are great at problem-solving. Empaths are highly imaginative and, as a result, tend to see certain things that other people can't quite conceptualize as easily.

- **Enthusiasm for life**

Our deeply emotional nature as empaths means that we experience things on a much deeper level. A walk in the park feels like much more than just exercise because we can absorb joy and positive energy from the surroundings. Your highs are much higher than those of the average person, and you find joy in even the little things. This means that you have an innate zest for life and that you can enjoy even small pleasures.

Most empaths are enthusiastic about life, and as a result, they are experience joy with a higher intensity. This reinforces their compassionate nature and desire to make the people around them happy as well. Enjoying life and pleasing others is the empathic mantra.

- **The Ability to Read other People**

  Empaths can see right through people's facades and straight to their true emotions and intentions. These elevated perceptions mean that you are quick to spot deception. You can stay away from negative people and energy. Empaths have sharp instincts and are excellent at reading body language and nonverbal cues that point to a person's truest nature and their motivation. People are unable to hide their feelings from you. You can easily tell when a friend is in distress, even when they are trying to mask their pain.

- **Empaths are Happy in their Own Company**

  While most people find solitude disconcerting, empaths find time alone, rejuvenating and relaxing. Human beings are social animals, but you are comfortable in your own company and can spend a lot of time alone without feeling lonely. Being with other people can be draining and nerve-wracking. Seek out time alone to relax and avoid emotional overload. It can take isolation and self-reflection to maintain your mental health. This means that you do not need the company of other people to be happy, which a gift that most of the population does not possess.

How to Embrace Your Gift

While being empathic comes with many gifts, it can also feel like you have the burden of saving the world on your shoulders. It can feel like you have the responsibility of making everyone else happy, even when it comes at the expense of your own wellbeing. Accepting your nature as an empath means that you will learn to embrace your gifts. You will also learn to guard yourself against the overwhelming emotional burden that others will attempt to shove off onto you. There is a balance to be struck between loving others and protecting yourself.

You can only make full use of your empathic gifts when you learn to accept your quirks, your oddities, and your sensitivities. Trying to suppress any of your qualities not only denies you the power to live your life fully but also denies others the benefit of your natural gifts. The key to embracing your empathic nature is in learning to love yourself and knowing that serving others does not necessarily mean disregarding your own needs.

To truly embrace your gifts and enjoy your natural abilities, the following techniques will come in handy:

1) *You come first.*

   If it helps, think of it this way. It is pretty difficult to pour from an empty cup. When it comes to empaths, there is a tendency to value the needs of other people over our own. Since we are so sensitive to other people's emotions, needs, and suffering, we tend to priorities their pain over our own wellbeing. This can lead to fatigue, exhaustion, and feeling emotionally drained.

Even in helping others, you need to first love yourself before you can attempt to love others. Letting people take advantage of your compassion or abuse your kindness is not helping them but enabling narcissistic tendencies. When you put yourself first, you have more energy to help others and derive more joy from it.

Make time in your schedule so that you can focus on your dreams and goals. Do not succumb to the desire to always be available or on-call for other people, while neglecting the things that matter to you. Being an empath is a gift, but you need to manage it in such a way that you do good to yourself in the same way that you cater to other people.

To live a full and empowered life in control of your gifts, you need to understand the difference between service and servitude. If you have centered your life around taking care of others, then you have programmed yourself to be in servitude to others. Use the same compassion that you feel outwardly, and turn it in upon yourself.

2) *Release negative energy.*

Even as empaths, there is only so much we can do. Taking up arms against all the problems in the world will just leave you feeling depressed, overwhelmed, and inadequate. Manage the amount of negative energy you absorb from situations, especially those that are beyond your control. When you cannot handle the kind of energy you are soaking up from those around you, you might be compelled to use coping mechanisms such as overeating, alcoholism, or other negative habits.

There will always be good and bad things in the world, you need to make a conscious decision to surround yourself with positive energy that does not wear you out or steal your joy. Learning how to feel emotions fully and letting them pass instead of holding on to them will help you in coping with your sensitivities and embracing your emotional nature. This is also a habit that promotes stillness within your mind, a vital ally for mental health.

3) *Find time to be alone.*

As an empath, people will be drawn to you. You are a good listener, a nurturer, and you make emotional connections easily. Naturally, people want to be around you. They come to you for advice, guidance, and comfort. However, if you keep absorbing and internalizing other people's feelings, you take on their energy and end up exhausted. To avoid this overload, setting time to be alone with your own emotions and taking the time to process them, will help you with staying balanced and in-touch with yourself.

When you are constantly surrounded by people, it becomes difficult to separate their emotions from yours. Solitude will help you rejuvenate and relax without constant onslaught from external sources. For an empath, time alone can be your biggest ally in staying in touch with your own feelings and needs.

4) *Getting away from social conditioning.*

For most empaths, the feeling that they are overly sensitive or moody has been drummed into them since they were children. Society has conditioned you to feel that you are odd and that if you do not behave in a certain way, then there is something wrong. The first step in using and embracing your empathic gifts requires that you put aside all the pre-programmed notions that make you want to suppress your sensitive and emotional nature.

Being an empath is a strength that you can use to empower yourself and others. Once you accept that you do not need to conform to societal expectations, you can truly tap into your innate powers and let your loving nature shine. Regardless of who you are, chasing universal acceptance will only diminish your gifts as you try to fit everyone's expectations. Shake off the mold that has been placed upon you and unleash your inner power with no reservations because you have a right to be who you are.

Gain Self-Confidence

As humans, we tend to define our value based on other people's opinions and perceptions. This can be especially significant for empaths whose sensitivity to other people makes them more prone to developing low self-esteem. So, the feeling that you do not fit in or that your caring nature makes you less-than is one of the constant struggles that an empathic person has to learn to deal with.

Yes, you might soak up the feelings of other people; however, that does not exempt you from taking control of your own emotions and outcomes. For an empath, it's very easy to play the role of the victim and allowing yourself to be influenced and controlled by the actions of others. Ultimately, they must learn to take responsibility for their own happiness. Every person must learn personal accountability to lead a successful life.

A key realization on the path of embracing your gifts as an empath is knowing how to distinguish between your feelings and the emotions that you are absorbing from others. When you can take charge of your own thoughts and life, then you can truly empower yourself with the gifts that you possess. To effectively take charge, you need to gain confidence in yourself, your abilities, and your place in the world.

These are some of the techniques you can use to boost your confidence and empower yourself:

1) *Acknowledge and accept that you are an empath*

Confidence comes from knowing who you are and accepting yourself. If you spend time and energy trying to suppress your empath tendencies so that you can conform or fit in, you are in effect undermining your own self-worth. Your sensitivities and emotional nature will always shine through, no matter how hard you try and disguise it. So, take a different approach and accept yourself, your strengths, your weaknesses, and everything in between because if you cannot find value in yourself, it will be impossible for anyone else to find value in you. Self-awareness and self-acceptance are the first steps in building your self-esteem and confidence.

2) *Trust your Intuition*

As an empath, you naturally have a very intuitive nature that gives you a sense of things that may not be obvious or visible to other people. It may be tempting to try and override this natural instinct in an attempt to seem more rational and logical. However, it is important to remember that it is this nature that makes you more creative and more innovative than other people. Having the gift of foresight and inner wisdom that guides should be one of the things you celebrate about yourself. Do not be afraid to follow your instincts or listen to your sixth sense. These attributes are the ones that guide you in making good decisions and staying on the right path.

3) *Don't play the victim*

We may not have control over the actions of other people, but we do have control over our own actions and the paths we choose. Staying in abusive or toxic relationships is a choice that you make. Knowing the difference between being compassionate and letting other people take advantage of you is a big step in realizing your self-worth. Our compassion has been given to us so that we might help other people. We are not given these gifts to enable narcissists or manipulators. If you resign yourself to always being the "giver" and allowing other people to keep taking from you, then you are in effect playing a victim instead of taking control of your emotions and your life.

4) Recharge

Empaths easily get lost in the process of helping others and ensuring they have attention to give their family and friends. Take a moment to recharge by spending some time on your own in soothing activities such as mediation will help you unwind and unload emotional baggage. Even machines need downtime, so you should not feel guilty if you need to get away from everything and everyone to recharge yourself. When you feel overwhelmed, find a way to rest and take back your power when you start to feel sensory overload. Meditation, spending time in nature, or simply creating a mental image of being in a bubble that keeps out negative energy are simple and easy ways to rejuvenate yourself.

5) *Set Boundaries*

Take note of how certain people and situations make you feel. If you have vampires in your life that seem to suck the energy out of you, it may be time to establish boundaries. Compassion is a natural instinct for the empath, but knowing when you've had enough and when it is time to take a step back from the negative and toxic energy will keep you emotionally and psychologically healthy. Your first responsibility is to yourself and your own mental health. You cannot be of any use to others if you are unable to take care of yourself. Separate yourself from the energy vampires, and surround yourself with the people and things that give you joy.

6) *Love Yourself*

This is perhaps the sum total of the principles above. It is easy for an empath to feel that loving themselves is a kind of selfishness or that they need to care for others more than they do themselves. Practice self-empathy, in the same way, you worry about and nurture other people, show the same kindness and compassion to yourself. Make sure you are physically and mentally healthy.

Self-empathy requires that you pay attention to your own feelings and thoughts. Take time to honor your feelings and pursue your own desires and go after the things that are important to you. Recognize that you can be vulnerable and strong at the same time. Always bear in mind that you can only transform the lives of others by living up to your full potential as an empath.

Chapter 4

The Gift of Empathy

Intuition is the empaths internal power to sense what is wrong and what is right. Everybody has a sixth sense, but in empaths, this innate ability is well developed due to the higher sensitivity to external energy and emotions. Your intuition will always guide you to a path that is true to your strengths, but often, we fight with it as we strive to maintain a logical and pragmatic approach to people, situations, and life in general.

As an empath, it is important to learn how to use and trust your gift of intuition. Sometimes that strange feeling that says "do this" or "stay away from him" may seem farfetched or unreasonable, but there is a healthy way to integrate your gifts of intuition and exceptional perception into your life while still maintaining a sense of balance. In order to trust the gifts that you have been given, you must first identify them.

Identifying Your Abilities

When it comes to intuition, empaths have abilities in different areas. Depending on where your strengths lie, you may fall into either one of the following categories;

Telepathic Empaths

Have you ever been sitting, pining over someone, or missing the voice of another person, and suddenly the phone rings, and it is the one you have been thinking about? Or have you gone to check on your children at night after feeling uneasy only to find them running a fever? Telepathic empaths intuitively sense what their loved ones are going through even if they are not in the same room or vicinity. These individuals establish such a deep connection with the people in their lives that they can sense when the other person is unwell. These bonds can stretch for miles and miles.

However, for telepathic empaths, it is important to recognize that your emotions can project as an intuition. For example, if you are afraid of being lonely, you might fight yourself constantly, feeling that your partner will leave you. This is not a true insight, but rather, a projection of your own insecurities. As a telepathic empath, your greatest gift is in your ability to forge a deep connection with others that gives you an insight into what they are feeling or thinking.

Precognitive Empaths

The abilities of precognitive empaths lie in their gift to foresee what is likely to happen in the future. They can receive premonitions consciously and subconsciously. Subconscious premonitions can occur in the form of dreams that turn out to be a prediction of things that will happen. Premonitions can also occur consciously where an empath gets into contact with a certain person or object.

As a precognitive empath, it is important to be responsible when revealing your premonitions to others. Well-meaning empaths can cause emotional distress to other people by revealing negative or scary premonitions that paint the future in a bad light. Succumbing to the idea that you are all-knowing or in control of future events is an abuse of your gifts. Premonitions should be shared only for the benefit of the other person and not as a show of power or an intimidation toll.

As a precognitive empath, it is easy to mistakenly think that you are responsible for making your predictions come true. This is not accurate. A precognitive empath simply serves as a conduit for communicating what might happen in the future and are not the directing force that determines the course of events. You should, therefore, not feel guilty if you have negative premonitions about a person.

Earth Empaths

There are empaths with an innate ability to detect changes and possible occurrences in the environment. For example, there are people who can sense if a thunderstorm is imminent, they can tell if there is going to be an earthquake and generally have an uncanny ability to predict natural phenomena. These individuals have an unbreakable connection to the natural world.

If you are this type of empath, you have the ability to absorb and decode the energy from the earth. You feel the different vibrations projected from the ground, in your body. An earth empath is naturally drawn to nature and feels most at peace when surrounded by it. This planet is intimately connected to your body. To keep your abilities at their peak and empower your intuition, you need to stay connected to the wild outdoors in one form or another.

Spend time in natural surroundings, take hikes in the green areas such as parks and forests, spend time sailing, and commune with natural elements to rejuvenate and recharge your spirit. You can also practice planetary medicine by doing your part in helping conserve and safeguard the environment. Fulfilling this purpose will help you in feeling content in your role as an earth empath.

Animal Empaths

If you have an ability to sense what other creatures need or what they are feeling, then you are an animal empath. You have a natural affinity for wildlife and pets; you can instinctively tell if they are in pain or distress. An animal empath will not only be drawn to fauna, but they will also be drawn to you in return. You understand that other living beings have the ability to sense our emotions and pick up on our energy.

Many dog lovers will tell you that their pets can tell when they are in a good mood and when they are feeling down and sad. Animals are also intuitive when it comes to human emotions and are able to detect when they are in the presence of an empath who can understand their needs. These individuals thrive when working in animal shelters or in professions where they can nurture and care for animals. This helps in enhancing and utilizing their natural abilities.

Self-Awareness

Ultimately, being aware of what your empath strengths are will empower you to live your life in full as well as help others with the gifts you possess. As empaths, we tend to mirror what everyone else's emotions are so that we can acquiesce ourselves for their comfort. We do this in order to be needed, and in the process, we tend to forget our own feelings. This is why self-awareness is a huge part of a thriving, for those with a sensitive nature. If you cannot make the distinction between your needs and those of other people, you will be likely to get lost in their world and take on personalities, energies, and emotions that are not yours. The net effect of this is that you will stifle your own goals to concentrate on other people.

To avoid self-sabotage, you should accept that empathy is a real thing. Emotions are transferable and can be picked up by other people as impulses. Those who absorb or soak up other people's emotions but doubt the reality of empathy will end up treating the external feelings as their own. Acknowledging your sensitivities may be difficult at first, but recognizing and accepting that your gift is real will guide you in how to best use your skills and avoid the pitfalls that come with compassion and contagious emotion.

Your empathy will not kill you, but it can make your life a lot more difficult if you are not able to identify and process it in a way that does not overwhelm or swallow you. Be receptive to your emotions, even when they are unpleasant. Learning how to feel, process and pass negative thoughts will keep you in control and mentally balanced. In most cases, for empaths, they tend to carry a lot of baggage from other people and being aware that everything you're feeling is not necessarily yours to carry, will enable you to cope adequately with your empath sensitivities.

In your journey, to uncovering and understanding your empath nature, you will need to;

- Uncover your own driving needs; this involves finding out what your desires and goals are. Ask yourself what is important to you without considering other people's needs or your sense of obligation to them. Find out what is that you want for your life.

- Uncover the unhealthy habits you use to get away from your feelings, whether it's overeating, alcoholism, or any other kind of escapist mechanism. Be truly honest in assessing how your emotional state impacts your behavior. This will be the first step in identifying the destructive habits you are engaging in as a result of the lack of a proper means to process and manage your thoughts.

- Seek the truth by asking yourself the following questions:
    - Is this emotion mine, or am I just projecting other people's emotions?

o How do I feel at this present moment? What energy is surrounding me, and how is it making me feel? Am I absorbing positive or negative energy from my surroundings?

o If I am in a negative environment that is affecting my energy, how can I change how I am feeling? What will make me feel better and help me calm my emotions? Is it solitude? A walk in the park? Meditation?

Career and Profession

Empaths are capable of thriving in the workplace. Their creativity, innovativeness, and ability to forge strong bonds serve them well in the professional field. However, due to the higher emotional sensitivity, they are also more prone to stress and anxiety, especially when they work in high-pressure environments. Empaths prefer independence to structure and are good at thinking outside the box since they see things differently from the average person.

In the right work environment, an empath will thrive and be empowered by the intuitions, creativity, and ability to connect and form good relationships with others. In contrast, the wrong workplace can stifle and limit them from fully accessing their potential and gifts. It is, therefore, important for you to consider the work environment you are in and how it impacts your emotional balance. To determine this, ask yourself the following questions;

- What fulfillment do you get from your job?

As an empath, you will be naturally better at meaningful work that involves helping people in one way or another. They have a natural instinct for compassion and finding a job that lets them utilize this instinct will be more fulfilling for them in the end. You should not be afraid to follow your passions and find professions that hold meaning for you, ultimately, you will be happier for it, and you will most likely excel at something you are passionate about.

- What kind of energy in terms of people and the environment are you surrounded by?

  You cannot get away from the fact that you soak up the emotions of the people around you and the energy of your surroundings. This means that if you are surrounded by negative people and energy vampires, every day at work will be emotionally and even physically taxing for you. Your hypersensitivity to feelings, as an empath, means that you will be more susceptible to picking up stress from other people. This will not only affect your productivity at work but may also have a negative impact on your psychological health.

To ensure that your professional success is not impacted negatively by your empathic nature, the following strategies will keep you productive while still maintaining your mental health.

First things first. Getting the right job will get you halfway to professional success. Pursuing something you're passionate about means that you will get enough fulfillment from your job, and you will always feel motivated to get up in the morning and get to it. However, it is not realistic to expect that we can always find the exact line of work that we are interested in, so it is important to have your options open and generally opt for careers that will enable you to take advantage your strengths such as compassion, intuition, innovativeness, or creativity. For any person, playing to your strengths is always the best strategy when it comes to personal development. As the cliché goes, if you judge a fish by its ability to climb trees, it will spend its life believing that it is stupid. If you know you like nurturing and caring for people or animals, pursuing a job in accounting is not going to do much for you. The trick is to find a job that gives you leeway to utilize your innate abilities and skills, and you will be much happier for it.

The best jobs for empaths include:

- Any work from home position that enables you to control your environment and the kind of energy you are exposed to.

- independent contractors, virtual assistants, software engineering, graphic design

- Songwriting, writing, painting or other creative arts

- Nursing, caregiving, doctors

- Working in charities or humanitarian programs and organizations.

Jobs that an empath should avoid:

- Sales

- Highly structured corporate environments

- Jobs that require constant travel

All in all, regardless of your line of work, you can take steps to ensure that you can cope with work and professional expectations as an empath without being overwhelmed by stress or negative energy. The following tips should ensure you stay productive and manage your environment adequately:

- Set clear boundaries. Even in the workplace, protect yourself from toxic people and drama junkies who drain energy and transfer their stress to you. Learn to say no when you feel you have had enough and focus on the positive people in your workplace.

- Don't overwork. As an empath, you will be tempted to try and please everyone but do not overwork yourself. Pace yourself and take regular breaks to avoid sensory overload or getting stressed out.

- Declutter your workspace. Working in a disorganized environment can create stressful energy, and research has shown that working in an environment without clutter has a calming effect on our emotions. Having a plant or inspirational plaques around your workspace may help make your area more serene.

- Whenever you feel like you are getting overwhelmed, deep breathing for some time will help in soothing and rejuvenating you. A simple breathing technique is inhaling to a count of six then exhaling for a count of six for about two minutes.

- Don't carry your work stress home. For empaths, It is difficult to separate their emotions, meaning that a bad day at work will follow them right back to their house. Learn to have fun outside of work and strive to have a vibrant social life that is separate from your professional world. Balance is key in life and making your profession or job the center of your existence is not psychologically healthy in the long run.

Personal Relationships

So, when it comes to love and sex. Empaths have the ability to establish deep emotional connections with their partners, stemming from their innate ability to understand the feelings of others. These individuals thrive in relationships where they feel secure in their partner's love and loyalty. That said, it is very easy for empaths to lose themselves in relationships and find solace in focusing only on the other person's needs and forgetting their own.

In intimate relationships, an empath is constantly faced with a struggle that tears them between wanting a partner and also feeling safer in solitude. They want to be loved but sometimes wish to avoid the emotional burden that comes along with companionship. In effect, empaths need a strong sense of self to avoid sabotaging their own relationships with their emotional hypersensitivity.

The upside of being in a relationship with an empath is that we tend to be so sensitive that we are in tune with our partner's emotions and can intuitively tell what they need. Sensitive individuals make great lovers and support systems for their significant others. On the downside, the more connected we are to someone, the greater the level of absorption of their emotions, which in turn leads to feeling emotionally drained and constantly worn out.

This, however, should not be taken to mean that empaths are incapable of having loving, fulfilling, and lasting relationships. It just means that they must become aware of their emotional sensitivities and how best to manage them within the relationship. Every hurdle can be overcome with enough effort to mitigate the damage. To determine if your empathic sensitivities have an impact on your relationships, ask yourself the following questions;

- I'm I easily hurt?

- Am I afraid of losing myself in a relationship?

- Am I susceptible to emotional contagion where I soak my partner's negative or positive emotions?

- Do I have difficulty asserting my needs?

- Am I able to establish boundaries in a relationship?

- Am I scared of confrontation and arguments?

- Do I feel the need to be alone sometimes?

- Does my partner talk on the phone while we are together, annoy me more than it should?

- Am I more comfortable sleeping alone sometimes?

If you answered yes to more than six questions, you have full-blown empathic tendencies in your relationship and may be required to learn how to manage your hypersensitivities in order to have a healthy partnership. These proclivities can, however, be effectively managed and should not interfere in your ability to create a lasting intimate connection.

The following strategies will inform you how to sustain a healthy relationship:

1. Do not take things personally.

   As empaths, we have a hard time processing and letting go of emotions. Our hypersensitivity to other people's energy and feelings means that we get annoyed too easily and for too long. While the average person will get angry and get over it in a short time, in relationships, sensitive individuals tend to get hurt easily and deeply.

   A misunderstanding can cause you to feel attacked or unappreciated, even when your partner means no offense. This overreaction means that as an empath, you can easily blow things out of proportion and escalate situations that can easily be resolved with proper communication. Try to be less reactive and take some time away from the situation to allow yourself time to assess it objectively.

2. Do not nag.

   Sometimes, when we feel like the other person is not listening to us, we tend to resort to repeating ourselves over and over.

Nagging just serves to push the other person away and makes them more resistant to you. Learn to manage your emotions by focusing on a single issue and not piling up all your emotions in one conversation. Overburdening your partner with a load of emotions can be exhausting for them, and the net effect of this is that your partner will start spending more time away from you because you are draining them.

3. Give each other breathing space.

    Developing a clingy or unhealthy attachment to your partner is detrimental to your relationship. Develop a life outside of your relationship so that you do not crowd your significant other or make them feel like they are responsible for your happiness. Develop your own interests, hobbies, and pursuits and give them room and time to also develop their passions. A healthy relationship is made up of two whole individuals, but when one partner needs the other to complete him or her, the other will feel overburdened and stifled by the lack of room.

4. Rejuvenate.

    Relationships take work and energy. Taking some alone time to decompress and process your feelings puts you in a better frame of mind. Soothing and relaxing activities such as yoga or meditation will help you to fill centered and manage your emotions. For empaths, alone time gives us time to get away from too much sensory input and rejuvenate ourselves. The more time you take to refresh, the happier you will be, and ultimately happier people make better partners than people who are constantly stressed and anxious.

5. Do not be a fixer.

   Empaths constantly feel the need to help and improve other people's lives. While this is a noble ideal, in a relationship, you should not play the role of the fixer. If you constantly feel the need to tell your partner how to be or what to do, you are sabotaging your love. People need support from their companions, not criticism, nor unsolicited advice. Resist the urge to offer suggestions or advice and instead just be there for your significant other.

   When you feel tempted to criticize or offer suggestions teach yourself to say, "I trust you to sort it out." This will also help you in avoiding soaking up your partner's stress. In the same way that you would like to be accepted as you are, let your significant other be true to themselves and don't try to change them to suit your ideals or mental image.

Community

Apart from intimate relationships, empaths also need to establish good connections with their friends and social circles. To live in harmony, we need to find a way to co-exist with other people in a way that we can build supportive relationships and strong bonds. By following the strategies below, you can have better social relationships and avoid toxic energies and emotional overload.

1. Limits and boundaries.

   As empaths, your natural compassion will make you want to always be there to help your friends, family, or other people in need. However, it is important to realize that you need to have boundaries that safeguard you from taking on too much emotional baggage from other people. Learning to say no can set you free from so many obligations that we push upon ourselves or that others have imposed on us. Avoid becoming a doormat yourself to people who take and take and never give back. Set your standards high and keep your circle small. Do not be afraid to cut off the people who take advantage of your kindness and compassion. Any relationship requires give-and-take from both parties; any other balance is unhealthy.

2. Avoid social vampires and toxic energy.

   Step away from whatever is upsetting or making you anxious. If you are in a loud party and the sensory input is too much for you, excuse yourself and go into a quiet place where you can get away from all the emotions surrounding you. If being in a certain place makes you uncomfortable, leave. You have the power to control the environment you find yourself in, and you do not need to subject yourself to negative emotions or toxic energies to please other people. Social vampires unload their emotional baggage on you and leave you exhausted and drained. Safeguard your own needs and control the kind of feelings that you are soaking up by ensuring you surround yourself with positive people and positive energy.

3. Distinguish between your emotions and those of other people.

An easy way to determine if you are projecting other people's emotions is to take note of how you feel around said company. If you notice that your mood changes suddenly when around someone or you start feeling a dip in your energy level, then you are projecting the emotions of the other person. Some people will have a negative impact on your thoughts and wellbeing, while others will make you feel better. Either way, it is important to know which sentiments are your own and distinguish them from the ones you are soaking up from other people.

4. Get plenty of sleep.

Sleep is not only good for your physical wellbeing; it is also a requirement for good mental health. Lack of rest makes us irritable and emotionally unbalanced. A good slumber is one of the ways that an empath can use to avoid fatigue. Shuteye can also rejuvenate the system. Due to heightened sensitivities, empaths spend most of their time feeling and experiencing deep emotions that can be exhausting. Sleeping gives you a well-deserved break from sensory overload and helps to keep you emotionally balanced and physically well.

Chapter 5

Empath's Sensitivities

As an empath, your hypersensitivities give you the innate ability to feel other people's emotions, sense things other people cannot, and develop a naturally compassionate nature that makes you an asset to humanity. However, these hypersensitivities also predispose you to soak up other people's stresses. Smells and noises have the tendency to become overwhelming to you. It can feel like walking around with the world's most eternal migraine.

When we get overwhelmed, we tend to self-medicate in an attempt to deal with the emotions that may be stressing us out. This means that empaths are susceptible to developing psychological and physical disorders as a result of their sensitivities either directly or indirectly. People run to their own coping mechanisms for a reason.

Unfortunately, compassion does not place you above the need to cope with your own thoughts.

Sensory Overload

To lead a healthy and productive life, you cannot just lock yourself away in a room and avoid contact with the outside world as a means of limiting sensory input. Your sensitivities should not impede your ability to go about your daily life or interact with other people. Social and professional lives are a big part of who we are, so as empaths, we have to find ways to deal with being overwhelmed so that we can go about our business without worrying about overstimulation or overexposure.

To get control over sensory overload, you first need to identify what triggers you. Some of the common triggers are;

- Crowds

- Loud noises

- Low blood sugar

- Conflicts or aggression.

- Chemical sensitivities

- Over socializing

Effective strategies that you can use when faced with such situations, or when you are feeling overwhelmed by sensory overload include:

➤ **Take a break.** When you start feeling overwhelmed, whether you are at work, at home, or in the company of friends, take a break and find a quiet place to rejuvenate. If you are in the office, you can walk to an empty room and sit quietly for a while. If you are at a party, step outside for some fresh air and calm you. The point is to unplug from the stimulation and give your senses a moment to cool down.

➤ **Walk.** It may sound simplistic, but walking is one of the best ways to stimulate your brain and get a hold of your emotions. Walking helps to clear your mind and gives you time to think things over. So, when you start to feel overwhelmed, take a stroll around the block, take your dog to the park, or any other activity that gets you on your feet and moving. It is always a good idea to incorporate exercise into your calming activities.

➤ **Limit socialization.** If you find groups intimidating or difficult to handle. Focus on one-on-one interactions. For instance, if you need to go out, pick one person who you feel comfortable with to accompany you. We all need human contact from time to time, so you can still engage with other people but avoid overstimulation by sticking to one or two people until you feel comfortable. Sometimes you will be in a situation where you cannot avoid social gatherings. For instance, if you have to attend an office party, you can single out one person to have a conversation with instead of engaging with a large group. Allow yourself to enjoy one-to-one contact with people.

➢ **Shielding**. We all know the people and situations that bring out our worst fears. Minimize your contact with toxic people and create a barrier between you and negative energy. Whether you need to visualize yourself in a protective bubble that negative energy cannot penetrate or simply cut off contact, knowing how to safeguard your emotional wellbeing is the key. This is a quick way to protect you from the bad intentions of others.

➢ **Self-care**. Taking care of your physical body is important for your emotional wellbeing. Ensure that you eat well-balanced meals and avoid junk and sugar in your diet. Get plenty of physical exercises, and remember that sleep helps you to rejuvenate and recharge.

Mental and Emotional Issues

Some of the mental and emotional challenges that an empath tends to deal with as a result of their hypersensitivities include;

A. Emotional burnout.

Your compassionate and understanding nature will inevitably draw people to you because you are a good listener, understanding, and helpful. However, when you keep dealing with other people's issues and emotions, you may end up getting emotionally drained. Being conditioned to only give is a quick way to become burned out and exhausted. You must learn to take time for yourself so that you are not acting only on the whims of others.

B. Emotional contagion.

An empath is like a sponge that is immersed in water; it soaks up the liquid until it is completely soaked. You will have the tendency to absorb other people's feelings meaning that you could be having a perfectly good day, but when you come into contact with a person who is stressed out, your mood immediately shifts. This kind of emotional transfer makes empaths especially susceptible to energy vampires and toxic friends and relationships. It will be tempting for those around you, to use you for pity and attention. You must be hyperaware of these desires in other people.

C. Feeling "too much."

As an empath, you will, at some point, be labeled as "melodramatic," "oversensitive," or too emotional. This is because you can't help it, you cry at movies; you are moved deeply by simply nondescript things and have a tendency to react strongly to what other people may consider non-issues. Your feelings run deep and easily moved by your senses. This means that there are times you will overreact or take things too personally. An empath feels before they think. Therefore, their emotions will always be the dominant force in their actions and behavior.

D. Sensory overload.

When you keep on absorbing the energies of your surroundings, the more you are exposed, the more overstimulated your senses become. This is the reason most sensitive individuals like spending some time alone as a way of limiting sensory input. For instance, big groups or crowds will wear you out because you will be absorbing so many emotions from multiple sources and might end up feeling frazzled and anxious because of the overstimulation of your senses. You may not even be aware that you are taking in all of this data, but groups of people will move you to feel stressed and panicked. Alone time is paramount.

E. Sensitivity to external stimuli.

Loud noise, strong smells, and other extremes are typically uneasy for the empath. In some cases, empaths can actually get physically ill when someone yells at them. This is because their senses are more sensitive than those of the average person. So, any kind of extreme inevitably causes a bigger reaction that makes them uncomfortable and agitated.

To understand if these challenges are impacting on your ability to live a normal and fulfilling life, ask yourself the following: if most of these scenarios are true for you, then you are letting your sensitivities rule your world:

- ❖ Am I prone to unexplained mood swings?
- ❖ Do I feel unsafe or uncomfortable in public places?
- ❖ Do I feel like I am constantly being criticized or singled out?
- ❖ Do I have a hard time making friends and feeling comfortable around other people?
- ❖ Do I suffer from chronic fatigue for no apparent reason?
- ❖ Do I constantly feel the need to isolate and shut the world out?

Empaths and Addictions

When we feel overwhelmed or unable to process what we are feeling, the natural way to deal with this is to look for an outlet that will enable us to cope with our emotions. While there are many empaths who find healthy ways to cope and manage emotions and stress, there are those who resort to destructive habits as a means to escape feeling too much or being burdened by the weight of feelings. Overeating, alcoholism, gambling, and even drug use can provide temporary refuge for those seeking to escape their reality.

These destructions, at best, only provide a temporary reprieve and, in the end, will cause more harm than good. If you find that you are prone to looking for ways to escape your emotions, you should realize that your feelings may be driving you to unsustainable habits and addictions. If you find yourself seeking comfort in food, drinking alcohol to numb your emotions, or shopping compulsively when you are stressed, you need to address your coping mechanisms.

The first step is identifying what habit you have developed to help you numb or avoid dealing with emotions. Do you find yourself eating even when you are not hungry and feeling better while you are doing it? Do you keep a bottle of whiskey in the house to help ease your mind when you are upset? Does shopping make you feel better even when you buy more than you can afford or stuff you don't even need? Self-reflection will help you in identifying if you have an addiction and what triggers it.

If you realize that you have a problem, joining support groups such as Alcoholics Anonymous should help you in learning to manage your habits. They will also provide you with a support system for getting past the tough times. Find a group near you that deals with your particular addiction. Twelve-step programs are effective because they put us in contact with people who are in the same situation and, therefore, provide the motivation to kick the habit. It is always helpful to know others who understand what you are going through. A shoulder to lean on may make all the difference between using and abstaining.

Addictions are a direct result of our inability to deal with stress, so minimizing the amount of stress in your life is a big step in managing your compulsive habits. Some stress management tips include;

> Avoid toxic people and energy vampires.
> Get enough rest.

- ➢ Surround yourself with positive people.
- ➢ Take up a stress-busting activity; meditation, yoga, jogging or other types of exercise are a good start.
- ➢ Acknowledge your emotions and avoid trying to bury how you feel.
- ➢ Get a support system. This can be in the form of friends, family, or a therapist.
- ➢ Set boundaries that will protect you from picking up other people's negative emotions.

Physical Orders

Empaths are prone to suffering from chronic fatigue and stress. They are susceptible to physical disorders that are associated with anxiety. These include autoimmune disorders and an overall reduction in the body's immune system, meaning that they are more likely to pick up ailments and infections.

The situation becomes even worse when you are a physical empath and find yourself picking up the symptoms of other people. For instance, you can develop unexplained issues that doctors are unable to diagnose or treat because the actual ailments that you are portraying are not your own. This can lead to you being considered a hypochondriac or being diagnosed with a sensory processing disorder.

Many physicians will opt to treat empath patients with antidepressants or antianxiety therapies because they feel that even their physical symptoms are more psychological than physiological.

While this kind of medication may be useful and effective in extreme cases, your first line of defense, when it comes to safeguarding your health, should be in avoiding picking up other people's ailments and stresses. This can be done by;

- Always try to establish if the symptoms you are feeling are truly your own as opposed to someone else's.
- Stay away from negative energy and toxic environments.
- Limit physical contact with those who are ill, especially if you are a physical empath.
- Get plenty of sleep to rejuvenate your body physically and psychologically.
- Practice self-awareness when it comes to your body.

Other People Problems

Your sensitivity as an empath will, at some point, mean that you will face challenges when dealing with other people. We live in social environments where we have to interact with people constantly day by day. Learning how to manage relationships with others will help to avoid social anxiety.

As an empath, it is easy to see yourself as an outsider or like you do not fit in. We, therefore, feel compelled to try and suppress our empathic tendencies to avoid being different. However, when you do not give yourself the freedom to be who you are, you are unlikely to experience true happiness or forge meaningful relationships. The best approach, therefore, is learning the strategies that will help you in managing your sensitivities without necessarily feeling the need to change or hide the person that you truly are;

Some of the strategies you can use to avoid social problems include:

- Avoid narcissists and energy vampires – one of the drawbacks of being an empath is that people can sense your compassion, and will take advantage of your kindness. Identify the people who drain you emotionally and infect you with their toxicity and avoid them.

- Surround yourself with positive people – happiness and positivity are contagious. The more you surround yourself with good people, the happier you will be. Choose your friends and associations wisely and keep your environment as clean as possible.

- Don't be afraid to walk away – empaths have a problem setting limits and boundaries because your nature is to think of others before thinking of your own needs. Do not be afraid to walk away from emotionally abusive relationships or remove yourself from bad situations. Your first responsibility is to your own well-being, so trying to please others at your own expense is counter-intuitive.

- Be kind to yourself – take care of your mind and body. Develop good eating habits, exercise, and get enough rest. If your body is unwell, you will not be emotionally balanced. Our physical and mental wellbeing are intricately connected, and if you disregard one aspect, the others will be affected as well.

- Take time alone – time alone is important. Do not feel pressured to always be surrounded by people. Take time off and enjoy the peace that comes with solitude.

- Do not overreact – as empaths, since we experience emotions so deeply, we have a tendency to take things personally. It is easy to overreact. Always remember that holding on to negative emotions or grudges will hurt you more than it will hurt the offending party.

- Practice relaxation techniques – empaths need to find ways to de-stress and manage emotional overload. Practicing breathing techniques, taking walks in nature, or simply sitting in solitude can make a big difference in your mental state. The trick is to find that activity that makes you feel calm and grounded then incorporate it into your daily routine.

Chapter 6

Empaths and Other People

Being an empath is, undoubtedly, a gift that empowers you to have incredible intuitive and emotional strengths. The hypersensitivities of an empathic individual, however, require that they remain mentally balanced and grounded to avoid getting overrun by personal and external forces. Therefore, you need to guard against becoming overwhelmed by your feelings.

Protecting Yourself

1. *Detachment*

For an empath, their biggest weakness and strength is soaking up other people's emotions. This means that depending on your surroundings, you can be deeply affected by other people's feelings and behavior. However, to balance out this tendency of soaking up energy from external sources, you will need to learn to detach yourself.

When you give away your power over your own life by letting other people control your emotions, you are operating on a reactionary level. When you put up barriers that separates other people's issues from your own, you can detach yourself and stop getting lost in other people's problems. Avoid trying to fix everything or taking responsibility for everyone else's issues. Once in a while, it is ok to let people find their own way so that they are not entirely dependent on you.

2. *Meditation*

Meditation helps you to get in touch with your inner self and balance out your emotions. Because of your sensitivities as an empath, sometimes it is hard to know what you actually feel because you are so entangled in other people's feelings. Peace of mind allows you to shut down external stimuli and focus all your senses internally. This helps you focus on your own emotions and avoid sensory overload.

The beauty of meditation is that you can practice it anywhere and anytime when you start to feel off-balance. Find a quiet place and practice stillness until you feel your sense of self getting stronger and clearer.

3. Journaling

"Dear diary" is not just for teenage girls. Journaling is actually one of the best ways to increase your level of self-awareness. There is just something about putting things down on paper that makes them somehow more real and easier to comprehend. Keeping a daily journal will help you keep track of what you are feeling and also how different situations affect your emotional state throughout the day.

By keeping a journal, you will start to notice patterns in your behavior that emerge when you are in certain emotional states. For instance, if you had a stressful day and ended up in a bar for a drink. If it's just one, there is no big deal. However, if you notice a trend when on the bad days you end up going drinking, it could point to the development of an escape mechanism. Similarly, you might notice that every time you interact with a particular person, you end up feeling anxious or stressed. In this way, your notes will help you in identifying bits and pieces of your life that you would have missed otherwise.

4. Yoga

Yoga is another great way to shut down external stimuli and focus on your inner self. The healing properties of this practice and its positive effects on your psychological health are numerous. Enrolling in class and finding the right kind of yoga for you can significantly change your outlook and give you a sense of balance. Any kind of physical activity helps us in taking a break from our emotions and focusing on our spiritual and physical well-being.

5. Visualization

Mental visualization can help you in creating a barrier against negative energy. Picturing yourself surrounded by a shield that is impenetrable to negative and toxic energy will enable you to avoid soaking up toxic and negative emotions from your environment. This is a method of creating a safe space and erecting walls that you may use to safeguard your peace of mind and avoid energy vampires.

Empaths, Emotion, and Health

Empaths need to have a clear understanding of how their emotions impact on their health. Physical empaths, for instance, can pick up the symptoms of other people and have them manifest in their own bodies. Emotional empaths can also get physically sick when they are overstimulated, for instance, yelling, or aggressive behavior can actually make them ill.

It is common for empaths to be diagnosed as hypochondriacs or neurotic because they may sometimes display symptoms or conditions that other people do not understand. This means that occasionally, conventional medicine will be unable to resolve your problems because they do not necessarily fit in any scientific mold or system. Therefore, when it comes to your health as an empath, one of the major elements you need to take into consideration is creating sufficient barriers that serve to protect you from absorbing or soaking up other people's stress, anxiety, depression, or even physical symptoms.

The first step is to actually determine if, indeed, you are picking up ailments and disorders from others. This self-test should help you in determining that.

Ask yourself the following questions:

➢ Do I tend to feel fatigued around people?

➢ Have I ever been close to someone ill and started to feel unwell?

➢ Have I had symptoms that could not be medically verified?

➢ Does yelling or being involved in stressful situations make me physically ill?

➢ Are there people who make me feel anxious or stressed in their presence?

➢ Do I feel inexplicably positive or happy around certain people?

➢ Do I often develop mysterious and unexplained ailments?

➢ Am I hypersensitive to certain foods?

These questions will help you determine if and to what extent your empathic tendencies impact your health. If you find yourself answering yes to most of them, then you need to learn to manage your hypersensitivity so that it does not weigh negatively on your wellbeing, both psychologically and physically.

Empathic illnesses result from the manifestation of other people's symptoms in our own bodies. While you can pick up symptoms that you did not have initially, such as experiencing a migraine when your partner is having one or a twin child exhibiting the same ailments as their sibling, in most cases, empathic illnesses tend to amplify conditions that we might already have. Some common empathic illnesses that affect those who are sensitive are:

- adrenal fatigue

- irritable bowel syndrome

- autoimmune conditions

- social anxiety

- various phobias (such as a fear of crowds)

- chronic anxiety, fatigue, or depression

- fibromyalgia

Adrenal Fatigue

This is one of the most common ailments that empaths suffer from. Symptoms of adrenal fatigue are; lethargic states, insomnia, and anxiety. These may be accompanied by physical pain. This condition is caused when the amount of stress that a person is experiencing is too much for the adrenal glands to regulate with its natural mechanisms. This means that anxiety, especially the kind we pick up from other people, depletes our adrenal glands resulting in the above expressions. To manage this condition, the following steps will be effective:

- ➤ Avoid stressful situations, and people who make you anxious or depressed.

- ➤ Achieve plenty of rest.

- ➤ Vitamin C and B will help in boosting adrenal function, so incorporate foods rich in these vitamins into your diet, and you can also take supplements.

- ➤ Destress-meditate, exercise, and take time to process your emotions to avoid chronic stress.

- ➤ Maintain a healthy diet and lifestyle to keep your body functioning optimally.

- ➤ Eliminate energy vampires from your life.

How to Stop Absorbing Other People's Distress

We have mentioned energy vampires throughout the book, but you might be asking yourself, how do you know when you are dealing with an energy vampire? Most of these individuals will share a few common traits. The following guidelines will help you determine whether you are dealing with someone who drains the life out of you.

When you are around an energy vampire, you will tend to feel:

- Exhausted for no apparent reason.
- Your energy levels drop
- Your mood shifts suddenly
- You will feel consistently bad around this individual
- You feel sickly and anxious out of nowhere
- Your confidence dips, and you start feeling self-conscious
- You suddenly feel uncomfortable and ill at ease.

Energy vampires come in different forms. The important thing to remember is that your partner, friend, or family member can easily be the culprit. You should not picture an energy vampire as some stranger out to get you, in most cases, our villains are people who are close to us and people that we interact with often. Perhaps the most damaging relationship an empath can get into is a partnership with a narcissist.

How to Protect Yourself from Narcissists

A narcissist is an individual who has an inflated sense of their own importance, an insatiable need for recognition and attention, and most of all, lack empathy for other people. These individuals think that they are the center of the world and, therefore, everybody else's needs should come after theirs.

Narcissists have an innate sense of entitlement and are the "takers" in a relationship. When it comes to personality, the narcissist is the exact opposite of their empath with their lack of compassion, selfishness, and lack of understanding for other people. Narcissists will exhibit the following traits;

- They are incapable of recognizing the feelings and needs of others.

- Manipulate others to get what they want.

- Expect others to do what they want without question or expecting anything in return.

- Expect and demand to have the best of everything.

- Think they are more important and superior to others.

- Need to be the center of attention, will monopolize conversation without giving the other person the chance to express themselves.

Narcissists are good at getting what they want because they are skilled charmers and manipulators. They will worm their way into your life, and before you know it, you are hooked and in a full-blown dysfunctional relationship. Empaths will get seduced by the promise of an emotional connection and a great relationship, but in the end, it will end up being used by the abuser.

Narcissists are good at keeping empathic partners under their control and in dysfunctional relationships. They will play upon your emotions and compassion, batter your self-esteem, and make you feel like you are at fault and finally make you feel like you are crazy for wanting to change. They have no concern for your well-being or happiness; in their eyes, you are there to serve their needs and give them whatever they need. People spend years and years of their life stuck in relationships with the abusers and find it very difficult to leave.

So how do you guard against the narcissist?

1) Take responsibility for your own needs and happiness. People pleasing and the ceaseless need to serve others will keep drawing narcissists to you because they see an endless opportunity to exploit someone for their needs. Learn to distinguish the difference between service and servitude. Stand up for yourself and set boundaries whether the abusive individual is your boss at work, your spouse, a friend, or a sibling.

2) Do not try to get approval or affirmation from a narcissist. Trying to convince or get them to see your point of view is an exercise in futility, at the end of the day, the only person they are concerned with is themselves. Don't try to change this person. Do not fool yourself into thinking that you can fix them. They are happily misusing you, so the only thing you can adjust is your own attitude. You need to find a way to grow enough self-esteem and self-love to severe ties with the abuser.

3) Work on your emotional independence. When you have a strong sense of who you are and what you stand for, the narcissist is no longer attracted to you because they realize that they cannot take advantage of you. When you stop people-pleasing and focus more on developing and growing yourself, the abuser stops being the center of your attention,

and they move on to the next victim who will cater to their needs.

Surrounding Yourself with Likeminded People

Now that we have looked at who you need to avoid, who are the best people for empaths to form relationships with. Like any other connection, these interactions should allow you the freedom to be who you are. You should have a mutual balance where you complement each other's strengths and support each other's weaknesses. In any partnership where you feel the need to stifle your natural instincts, you can never be fulfilled or happy.

While life is not a fairy tale where you will find a perfect match and establish absolutely ideal relationships, there are people who make great partners for empaths. Some of these types of personalities are:

1) *Intellectuals and Thinkers*

While the strength of the empath lies in their emotional and intuitive nature, the intellectual operates on logic and reason. This means that he complements the sensitive partner by being strong in the areas where the other is weak, while the empath brings out the emotional sensitivity of the intellectual.

Intellectuals are at ease in their thought and are not as deeply in tune with their emotions as their counterparts are. As an empath in a relationship with a thinker, expressing your needs clearly will help you establish a connection with the rational half of the pairing. Intellectuals are good at coming up with solutions and will respond positively when you share your emotions and challenges with them.

2) *Empaths*

It is easy to assume that you will be best understood by someone who shares your empathic tendencies. This is not always the case, while it is not impossible to have a good relationship with a fellow emotional savant, there are bound to be complications in establishing healthy boundaries and understanding your own feelings. You will both have the inclination to absorb the personalities and moods of one another. Each person must be able to recognize their own needs and their partner's needs for the relationship to flourish.

3) *The Strong and Quiet*

If you are looking for the opposite of an empath, this personality is probably it. They are composed, solid, and consistent. You will not feel insecure or threatened when you are in a relationship with this person. They are not good sharers and are, therefore, unlikely to drain or overwhelm you with their own baggage. On the other hand, an empath is good for the silent type because they can help draw them out emotionally.

Chapter 7

Developing Your Empath Skills

Listening

When it comes to communication, empaths are good at picking up on the true emotions of people by reading their body language, using their intuition, and sensing the feelings of the other person. By soaking up the energy and thoughts of others, a sensitive individual is able to deduce energies that may not be apparent to everyone else. This makes it easy for them to understand the needs of others and their feelings.

Empaths have an innate need to try and make things better and fix problems for other people. While this is not necessarily a bad thing, it may interfere with the ability to listen to others because we become so focused on giving advice and making suggestions, we forget to let the other person express themselves. It can take effort to avoid jumping in with ideas and suggestions when people are sharing their views with you. This tendency can hinder effective communication, so empathic individuals need to learn to listen and listen with boundaries.

Good listening with boundaries.

Strategies to improve your empathic listening skills include:

> ➤ The LSF technique.

  The LSF technique refers to Listening, Summarizing, and Follow-up. Using this formula will help you to really understand and internalize what the other person is saying. The first step is listening, where you give the other person the time and space to express themselves. Try not to interrupt, and just take in what they are saying. The second step is summarizing in your mind the information the person is giving you. The next part involves paraphrasing and repeating what you have heard to the person so that they can recognize that you have understood their point. Take note of the person's body language when they are communicating, as this will provide further insight into how they are feeling.

> ➤ Use open-ended questions to prod and prompt.

  We learn more when we are listening than when we are talking. Prompting and prodding the other person with open-ended questions that go beyond a yes or no answer are bound to get you more information than simply listening without seeking clarification. Using questions such as "How did that make you feel?" or "What do you suggest we do about that?" are examples of true empathic listening.

➢ Refrain from making suggestions or offering advice.

As an empath, your natural instinct is to jump in with a solution and fix the problem. Resist this urge and just listen to the other person while questioning them for their ideas and suggestions. Do not feel the need to take on the situation solely and give the other person time to come to a conclusion. If they really need your help, they will ask for it.

➢ Be patient.

Empathic listening entails giving the other person sufficient time to express their views. Doing so requires patience. When you rush or pressure the person, they will become anxious and will lose the ability to express them clearly. Patience puts the other person at ease and enables them to open up to you without reservations. Even when you are tempted to interrupt with your own opinion, hold on to your thoughts and let the other person finish making their point. When you show people respect, they are bound to reciprocate when it is your turn to express your view on the situation at hand.

➢ Understand the power of silence.

Silence in a conversation will allow the individuals involved time to reflect and internalize what has been said. As much as quietness can be uncomfortable or awkward, resist the urge to fill every pause with words. Sometimes stillness can speak volumes.

Empathic listening is a useful skill in both professional and personal communication. In the workplace, people have diverse views, and taking the time to understand and listen to your colleagues' points of view is not only a sign of respect but also fosters good working relationships. Realize that everybody's perspective is important and, therefore, has a right to be heard. In personal settings, empathic listening will help you understand where your partner is coming from and what their needs are. Compassion may drive you to try and fix everybody's issues, but learning to take in information will help you in detaching and establishing a filter for other people's problems. When you practice active listening, you give the other person the chance to come to their own conclusion and come up with a solution.

Empowering a Person While Empowering Yourself

As an empath, you are compassionate and giving. You want to make everyone around you feel better. The one thing we forget is to take care of ourselves as well. Your gifts should empower you just as often as you use them to help others. *It is impossible to pour from an empty cup* as the cliché goes, meaning that you must first be kind to yourself before you can offer yourself to another person. Loving yourself is imperative and should be your priority before trying to love another.

Strategies for empowering yourself;

1. Self-awareness – take time to know your needs and feelings. It is easy to get lost in other people's desires. You have an internal drive to make everyone else happy. Find out what your own passions are and what fulfills you; find a way to pursue your own goals. The more satisfied you are as a person, the better you will be in your work, relationships, and other roles.

2. Lean into your intuition – it might be tempting to suppress your empathic sensitivities in order to conform to other people's expectations or fit in. Your keen Intuition and ability to sense things are gifts that you should utilize for your own good and the betterment of others. Trust your gifts and use them as a path to the inner wisdom you are capable of possessing through your compassion.

3. Find the right job - Your career will play a big role in you achieving your desires and emotional fulfillment. Empaths are born to nurture and heal. Therefore, do not go against your natural abilities or passions. For instance, if you are an animal empath, working in a profession that enables you to work with wildlife will allow you to fully tap into your compassionate gifts and provide you with so much more satisfaction than being stuck behind a desk somewhere.

4. Surround yourself with positive things - Picture yourself as a sponge that will soak up whatever is in its environment. Empaths are hypersensitive to external emotions and energy and, therefore, whatever it is you expose yourself to will impact your mental state. Positive people and environments will have an uplifting effect on you. Avoid negative nancy's and keep your feelings on the positive side to avoid picking up other people's stress and anxiety.

5. Rejuvenate and recharge - As an empath, we are bound to experience emotional and sensory overload from time to time. De-stressing and taking time away from emotional and sensory triggers will help you stay balanced so that you can reduce overstimulation. There is no limit to the number of things you can do to rest and refresh. For some, stillness and time alone work to solve these issues. Yoga and meditation can be strong allies in the quest to relax and unwind. Find what works for you and make it part of a routine that will give you an outlet when energy becomes overwhelming.

Empowering other people comes naturally to the empath, we are inclined to be compassionate and considerate of others. You can use your gifts to empower other people by:

1) Compassion - Your ability to sense and understand other people's feelings and needs means that, as an empath, you are

uniquely qualified to help those who are in need. You have a talent when it comes to sensing people's distress even when other people cannot do so. You can use these gifts to reach out and offer support to those who are hurting, in pain, or just need someone to listen to them. Empathic individuals make the best friends and companions because their natural intuition gives them insight into other people's emotions.

2) Intuition. - Your intuition is a tool that can help you foresee things that might happen and you can use this information to guide others. In the same way, your sixth sense helps you to avoid trouble and detect possibly dangerous situations, and you can use this to help those around you in avoiding disaster and damaging decisions.

3) Creativity - Empaths are great at coming up with ideas that other people may not be able to. This is because they are emotionally driven; they have a unique way of looking at tasks and obstacles. Your creativity as an empathic individual will be a great asset in the workplace and in coming up with innovative solutions to people's problems. The key is to trust yourself and to not be afraid of speaking up and putting your ideas into action.

Grounding, Clearing and Realizing

Empaths need to maintain an emotional balance to enable them to avoid getting overwhelmed by feelings and hypersensitivities. There are several ways to achieve harmony in your mental state. Most of these techniques are centered around limiting external energies and focusing inwards. Grounding is one such method that can help an empathic individual feel evenly distributed and in control of their emotions.

Grounding helps you feel connected to the earth. By touching the soil with your feet, your release your pent-up emotions and stress and take in the planet's healing energy through your soles, and this healing then travels up your body. Scientifically, establishing contact with the earth has been proven to have a calming effect on the nervous system.

The best way to experience grounding is by walking barefoot in a natural environment. Your feet should be in direct contact with the earth, whether you will be standing on a patch of grass or just walking barefoot in nature. Many reflexology and acupuncture spots are found on our feet, meaning that they are an effective pathway for releasing stress. When you walk with no shoes, you are inadvertently activating these reflexology points and allowing the release of pent up emotions.

You can also achieve the balancing effect of grounding through visualization.

When emotions become overwhelming or you are experiencing a sensory overload, take time to recharge and shut down sensory input. Find a quiet and isolated place, then just use a simple breathing technique as a way of focusing your attention inward. Taking deep breaths and feeling the breath enter and leave your body will help clear your mind.

Once you achieve tranquility, visualize yourself as anchored to the ground by your feet. Picture the negative energy that is leaving your body through your soles and the healing energy of the earth, imbuing your being. This visualization technique will enable you to feel grounded, regardless of where you are. It comes in handy when you are not able to go out into nature.

When it comes to clearing, the following techniques will help in getting rid of negative energy and cleansing yourself of negative emotions.

- ➢ Use journaling, music, or painting -express and process your emotions through art.
- ➢ Sever the cord to the negative energy -avoid or get rid of the negative energy by cutting the relationship off.
- ➢ Create a safe space for yourself where you can express your emotions freely.
- ➢ Spend time in nature.
- ➢ Detox using water – baths are a great way to relax and destress
- ➢ Plan alone time to rejuvenate.

Develop Your Emotions

When it comes to your emotions, learning how to manage them will enable you to maintain a sense of mental balance. As empaths, we tend to feel too much and too long. This means that we may have a hard time letting go of feelings and tend to have hangovers, where energy continues affecting you long after the event that triggered it has passed. When it comes to harnessing your power, your ability to manage your thoughts will play a big role in learning to live within your strengths without succumbing to sensitivities.

These are the tools you should use in developing your emotions:

- ❖ Accept yourself

- ❖ Prioritize your needs above the needs of others.

- ❖ Feel your own emotions and tune-in to your intuition. Always take time to assess and identify which feelings you are picking up from other people.

- ❖ Have filters and barriers that will safeguard your emotions from getting entangled with other people's feelings.

- ❖ Do not let other people's emotions or energies influence or change how you are feeling.

- ❖ Acknowledging the feelings that are not yours and clearing the energy away.

Overcoming Your Fears

It is not unusual for empaths to experience social anxiety. This anxiety arises from the intense emotions that empaths experience when interacting with other people. Imagine a scenario where you have been looking forward to going to a party for a while. When D-day arrives, you are excited and determined to have a good time. This all goes out the window as soon as you walk into the room and see all those people. Suddenly you are like a deer in headlights. You feel anxious and ill at ease and you start wondering what's wrong with you.

For many empaths, this kind of scenario is a common occurrence. To avoid or limit your social anxiety, the following strategies will be useful:

> Use mantras and affirmations – affirmations can help you to boost your confidence and avoid letting emotions get the better of you. If you are in a situation where you start feeling anxious or afraid, use empowering mantras such as "This stress and negativity are not mine, I release them and breathe in love."

> Self-awareness – when you are not aware of your own emotions, you are more likely to be reactive and susceptible to picking up other people's energies. Focus on your feelings and thoughts. For instance, in the scenario above, focus on having a good time and not what other people are experiencing and thinking. When you are self-aware, you can consciously shut down reactive emotions that cause you to feel anxious.

> Don't take anything personally – being hypersensitive means that we are deeply affected by other people's thoughts and opinions. Social anxiety partly stems from the fear of being judged by others. So, to overcome this anxiety, do not take everything so personally, and understand that people's

opinions should not affect your reality. Have a strong sense of self-value that is not deeply moved by negative emotions or the words of others.

Chapter 8

Empath and Emotional Intelligence

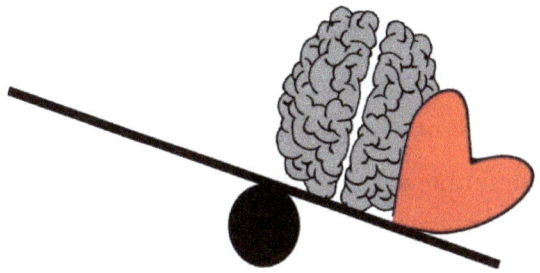

Emotional intelligence is the ability to understand and control emotions, coupled with the capacity to study and manage other people's feelings and desires. This interpersonal insight is a major determinant for success both in personal and professional endeavors. It is also telling of our ability to take control of our own behavior. This skill influences the kind of relationships we are able to establish with other people.

Emotions are at the core of human experience and are the psychological reactions that we have subconsciously to different stimuli. These feelings are typically characterized by three components;

- The subjective experience of the stimulus that triggers the reaction.

- The physiological response to the trigger such as sadness, anger, joy, or fear

- Behavioral response or expression of the psychological response.

When we come into contact with a person, experience or situation, our senses (touch, sight, sound, smell, or taste) transmit a signal to our mind. This data is transmitted via the spinal code and is first delivered to the limbic system. The limbic system is responsible for the generation of emotions and will decipher the signal as a feeling, first, before the signal is then forwarded to the frontal lobe of the brain. There, it is then interpreted logically. This pathway of processing stimuli is completely natural and occurs on a subconscious level, so we have no control over it.

If your friend hides behind a dark corner and jumps out to startle you suddenly, you are likely to recoil, shriek and possibly shout out in fear. In this case, the subjective experience is being startled. This is then followed by the feeling of terror which is the psychological response and then the behavioral expression of this fear which will cause you to draw back and scream

In essence, emotions are initiated by stimuli that we come into contact with. These stimuli can be people, experiences, memories, or thoughts. Once our feelings are triggered, they then cause or direct a behavioral response that is an outward expression of our instantaneous impulses. This is how our behavior and actions are influenced by our emotions.

Emotional Mastery

Emotional intelligence is comprised of two main competencies: personal and social. Simply put, emotional intelligence stems from the ability to understand and manage our own feelings. Through the ability to study our own reactions and responses, we will gain insight into the thoughts and desires of others. This knowledge can be used to manage our relationships with other people.

To understand this discipline, we need to look at the elements that make up the competencies of an emotionally intelligent person. The two elements at the core of personal competencies when it comes to this skill are self-awareness and self-control. On the other hand, the elements that make up social competencies are social awareness and relationship management.

We can summarize the elements of emotional intelligence as per the

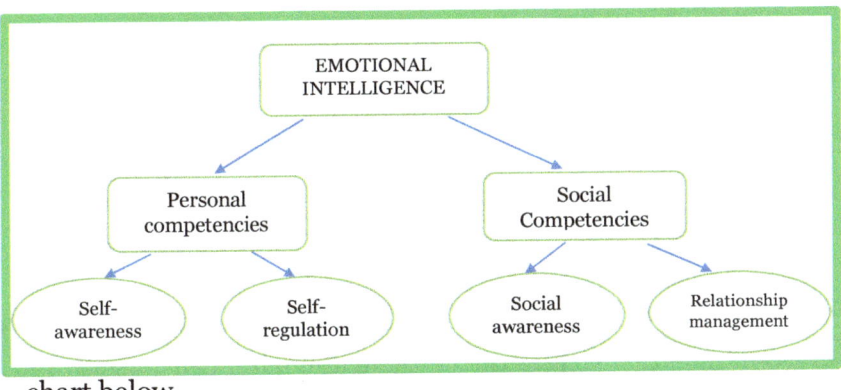

chart below.

Self-Awareness and Self-Regulation

Emotions occur as a reflex that we have no control over. When a subconscious reaction is going on, sometimes we might not even be aware of why we are feeling the way we are or what triggers us to think or react in a certain way. Self-awareness is the ability to recognize your own emotions and understand what is causing these responses in your brain.

Operating on emotional autopilot, where you are not in tune with your own feelings or your triggers, ultimately means that you will have no control over your decisions, actions, or behavior. For instance, if sadness causes you to overeat, unless you understand why you are feeling sad, you will be helpless in stopping the comfort eating. You must come to comprehend the point of origin, in order to sever the cord.

Taking the time to understand how you are feeling, what is causing this reaction and what you can do to alter this chain of events, is a big step toward social awareness. Some strategies you can use to increase your level of self-awareness are:

> ➢ There are no good or bad emotions, view your emotions objectively.

> ➢ Identify the things that make you feel a certain way or your emotional triggers.

> ➢ Pay attention to the thoughts you focus on and how they affect your mood. Dwelling on negative thoughts can push your brain into reacting in unfavorable ways.

> ➢ Seek feedback from others.

Self -Regulation

Once you have an understanding of what your emotions are, the next step is learning to manage them so that they do not affect or influence your behavior negatively. Back to our example of comfort, feelings can drive you to compulsive habits, especially when you do not know how to process or manage your own impulses. Self-control is the greatest management tool when it comes to steering your own actions.

Mastering self-control is a discipline that will enable you to reach your goals and live a fulfilling life. If you cannot control your emotions, then you cannot have any kind of say over the other aspects of your life. Addictions, socially unacceptable behavior, depression, and chronic stress are all manifestations of poorly managed feelings. You have the power to decide what sort of person you wish to be.

Some effective strategies for self-regulation are:

❖ Do not react in the heat of the moment, take a minute, step back and wait. You can use a simple "counting to ten" technique, taking deep and slow breaths or meditation until you feel you are in control of your emotions.

❖ Sometimes we are not aware of the thoughts that we run on a loop in our minds. Realize that the thoughts you focus on will influence how you feel. If you are always focused on all the bad things in your life, you are bound to be chronically stressed and anxious.

❖ When you feel your emotions are getting the better of you

write down an emotion vs. logic list. For example, if you are tempted to give your boss a piece of your mind, first sit down and write what giving in to your impulse will get you vs. what a logical approach could result in. This is a great way of putting things in perspective and helping you avoid overreacting by allowing you to weigh your options, logically.

❖ Do not make emotional decisions, i.e., do not make decisions when you are either extremely happy or extremely angry.

❖ Adapt. Change is inevitable and resisting; it is one of the major reasons that people lose control over their emotions. Adapt to your environment and expect that things will always shift; no situation will stay negative forever. Everything in life is transient.

Social Awareness and Relationship Management

When it comes to emotional intelligence- social awareness and relationship management will determine how competent we are around other people. In the same way that we experience our own feelings, others also have unique emotional reactions that determine how they relate to us and how well we understand them. Without social awareness, you will not be able to form good relationships because you will have no idea how to treat other people.

Routinely, you will be required to interact and form connections with other people. This occurs both on personal and professional levels, therefore, how well you understand the people in your life will determine to a great extent the kind of relationships you are able to forge. Quality partnerships come from individuals who are able to reflect and adjust the way that they communicate with others.

Good relationships are the key to success in the workplace. In any situation where you need to work well with people from different backgrounds, who may have different perspectives and views, your level of social awareness will determine how well you do. Being able to view situations objectively to better determine your communication methods, will allow you to move seamlessly through different environments.

Many people have lost their jobs, quit, or simply watched their productivity fall apart because they are not able to relate well with others. Acrimonious relationships will not only affect your psychological state but will also impact your ability to complete your tasks properly. This is why emotional intelligence is considered one of the most important factors for success in the workplace. The entire intellectual prowess in the world will do you no good if you cannot work harmoniously with others.

Some useful strategies for enhancing your level of social awareness and relationship management skills are:

1) Practice active listening.

2) Be present at the moment; avoid distractions when interacting with others. You may miss important cues that point to their emotions. Understanding feelings is paramount

for relatability.

3) Observe body language. Our bodies betray our innermost feelings, watching out for body language cues will help you understand other people.

4) Put yourself in the other person's shoes, i.e., use your empathic abilities to understand the other person.

5) Always seek for feedback and get other people's opinions and views.

6) Listen to your instincts.

7) Take time to build rapport with people – this will make them open up to you.

8) Be accessible.

9) Take criticism feedback well.

10) Do not be overly critical, give constructive criticism where necessary.

11) Remember the small things – call people by name, remember your boss's birthday, call your friend on their anniversary. Small gestures show that you value and appreciate other people.

Steps to Emotional Mastery

Step 1: Identify your emotions.

As an empath, your emotional hypersensitivity means that there are times when you will be overwhelmed by feelings from different sources. Take a moment to sort out your own thoughts vs. the ones that you have absorbed from others. Falling into a panic can make it even more difficult to separate yourself from others; everything can become messy and tangled.

Focus inward and ask yourself:

- What am I feeling?

- Why am I feeling this way?

- What is causing this emotion is internal or external?

- What can I do about it?

Step 2: Acknowledge and Appreciate Your Emotions.

Burrowing your head in the sand, looking for an escape mechanism or disguising your feelings will get you nowhere. Once you have identified what you are feeling, acknowledge and accept the impulse. Emotions are the psychological messages that our brain sends us. Be objective and realize that the thoughts you are experiencing are neither bad nor good. They are simply your brain's way of communicating to you so that you know how to respond to the external stimuli.

Step 3: Understand the emotion.

Get to the why of the emotion. Why am I feeling this way? What has triggered me to experience this? All feelings are reactions to some kind of stimuli. If you are to master them, you need to understand their cause.

- Consider these questions;

- What is this emotion telling me?

- What do I need to do as a result?

- Is this how I want to feel?

- Can I change these emotions?

Step 4: Awareness.

Confidence in you is an important part of emotional mastery. Trust your ability to handle the feelings no matter how negative they seem. Do not let your impulses overwhelm you, look at them objectively and build awareness in yourself that you can call upon to deal with the situation at hand.

Consider the following questions:

- Have I felt this way before?

- If yes, how did I handle it?

- Have other people been in the same situation?

- What can I learn from them?

- What options are available to me?

Step 5: Action

Take control of your emotions by taking action. Come up with a suitable plan to handle the wayward feelings. For example, are you reacting this way because of someone else? Is your environment stressing you out? Have you lost something that is causing thoughts tainted by sadness or anxiety?

Whatever the case is, get a plan to help you change your situation and how you are feeling. If you have handled a situation like this before, use your experience. If you have not dealt with something similar previously, you can consult other people for support.

As long as you are doing something to remedy the situation, the action and plan itself will make you feel much better and increase the feeling that you are in control of what is happening.

Step 6: Gratitude

We learn from our experiences and even the worst things that happen can teach us something about ourselves and about life. Be grateful for being able to take action and change your outlook. Learn from the mistakes in your past

Emotional Challenges for The Empath

Isolation

Empaths tend to experience loneliness because their sensitivities cause them to isolate themselves from people. To avoid being overwhelmed by other people's emotions, a sensitive individual will sometimes prefer spending time alone and may even become introverted. This hermit-like nature can mean that you are no stranger to feeling alone.

When you start to feel lonely or that you lack social contact, the following strategies can help you in overcoming this emotion.

- Do not be afraid to reach out, get out of your comfort zone, interact with people, and push yourself to open up more.
- Identify what kind of connection is best for you; do you prefer one on one interaction? Are you okay with group socializing, etc.? Start with the scenario in which you are most comfortable and gradually grow from there.

Discomfort

Feeling ill at ease is your subconscious trying to tell you that something is not right; in this case, you can either change your actions or change your perception. Discomfort comes from many sources; it could be boredom, social anxiety or physical pain. Whichever the case, your aches are meant to motivate you to change the situation or change your mind about the ordeal.

Some techniques you can use to deal with discomfort are:

- Identify what is causing the discomfort.
- Identify what you want instead.
- Change your actions to alleviate the discomfort.
- Change your mindset and accept the situation.

Disappointment

As an empath people's actions will hurt us deeply because our emotional sensitivity is very high. Knowing how to manage your expectations when dealing with other people will help you in managing disappointment. Feeling let-down is a normal part of life because we cannot always get what we want.

When you feel disappointed by yourself or other people, the following strategies will help you cope.

Strategies:

a) Learn from the situation and improve yourself.

b) Establish new objectives to keep you motivated.

c) Be patient, some setbacks are temporary and you will eventually get what you want if you do not give up.

d) Do not let your experience dim your positivity or affect your expectations of the future.

Fear

Empaths suffer from different kinds of fear. The worry of not fitting in, the familiar pain of social anxiety, the nervousness associated with sensory overload, among many others. These concerns can be an immobilizing factor that prevents you from going after your dreams. When you give in to dread, you lose your power of action. Agitation is a natural human emotion, but the trick is to feel the fright and do it anyway. As the cliché goes, the things you want the most live on the other side of fear.

So how do you deal with fear?

- -Identify what you are afraid of and why.

- -Prepare yourself mentally.

- -Come up with a plan of action

- -Trust yourself

Inadequacy

An empath takes it upon them to solve the problems of other people. When they do not succeed in doing this, feelings of inadequacy crop up. When you speculate that you have failed someone or let them down in some way, you begin to feel inadequate and start losing your self-confidence.

Be kind to yourself and understand that there will always be situations that are beyond your control. Do the best you can with what you have and take comfort in knowing that you have played your part. You can only learn from your mistakes and continue to try your hardest.

Emotional Overload

As an empath, you may experience so many emotions at once that they overwhelm you. When you try to process so many feelings at the same time, you will inevitably get overloaded and stressed out. It is important to prioritize your fears and thoughts and then address each separately. If you are feeling annoyed by several things, just look at each case independently. It is easier to solve problems when you look at them individually than when you try putting all your concerns in one basket.

Strategies to avoid emotional overload:

a) Decide what is important and what isn't.

b) Write down a priority list and tackle it one item at a time.

c) Focus on what you can control.

Chapter 9

Empathy Ongoing: Your Tools at A Glance

Hailey's Empath Experience

Before I had a word to describe what I was feeling and the turmoil that was my constant psychological state, I simply felt overburdened and weighed down by emotions I could not describe, even to myself. One minute I was ecstatically happy the next I was drowning in unexplained sorrow. What made it worse was that my parents thought I was attention-hungry and would often tell me to 'settle down."

I had no idea that other people did not go through this emotional roller coaster. I simply assumed that everyone was like me. However, the older I got, the more I realized that my friends were not quite as affected by things, as I was. They could have an altercation and it would be all but forgotten, while for me, emotional hangovers meant that I would still be mulling over an incident months after it happened.

Finally, when I was old enough to get some therapy, I discovered that there was nothing wrong with me. All my hypersensitivities just made me different, not abnormal. This discovery has liberated me to be myself without fear of being judged or not fitting in. I have embraced my empath nature, and now I just increase my knowledge on how to empower myself and get the best out of my abilities. My journey to self-acceptance has been slow and winding, but I wouldn't change a single thing about me now.

There are many uplifting stories of empaths who have managed to get past their fears and embrace their gifts and natural abilities. With the right tools, you should be able to live a happy, fulfilled and meaningful life, even with your sensitive nature. Before we get into the tools that will serve you in your journey of self-discovery, let us take some time to get centered and identify the intentions and goals we want to achieve through this process.

Identify Your Goals and Intentions as an Empath

Find a quiet place and sit in a comfortable position.

Have a pen and paper close.

a) Get into a meditative position with your spine, neck, and head aligned but relaxed.

b) Close your eyes and slowly focus all your energy inward.

c) Breathe in slowly to a count of six, as you breathe in; concentrate on feeling the breath go into your body.

d) Exhale slowly to a count of six again, focusing your attention on feeling the air leave your body.

e) Repeat this breathing technique for 3 minutes until you start to feel, relaxed and calm.

f) Don't worry if it takes you longer to feel centered, simply continue with the breathing technique until you feel completely calm.

Now get your pen and paper and write down your answers to the following questions, be completely honest with yourself and write down your innermost thoughts.

❖ Do I identify as an empath?

❖ What empath traits do I have?

❖ In which areas of my life do I need to feel more empowered? How so?

❖ What are my empathic strengths?

❖ Have I been using my abilities to empower myself and others?

❖ What has been stopping me from using my gifts and abilities so far?

All empaths are different in terms of their natural abilities. Some of the challenges they face may be common; some are unique to each individual depending on their situation in life. Therefore, the exercise above is meant to guide you in determining which of the tools of empowerment (that we shall get into) are most suited for you based on your own specific needs and challenges.

Step 1: Know Your Sensitivities

An empath is bound to be hypersensitive to emotions in their environment. Your ability to sense the feelings and thoughts of others means that you can connect easily with people. This bond also means that the undercurrents, energies, and intentions of others have the ability to affect you in dramatic ways.

Self-awareness and identifying the things that trigger your sensitivities will be the key in your being able to cope with your gifts and the pitfalls of feeling *everything*. If you are a physical empath, it means that you can feel other people's aches and pains in your body. You will need to establish boundaries to effectively protect yourself from picking up other people's ailments and symptoms. If you are an emotional empath, you will find that you pick up people's emotions and, at times, find it difficult to distinguish between your own thoughts and those of other people.

Knowing you are an empath is the first step. You will then need to dig deeper and find your particular sensitivities and the things that trigger you, both emotionally and psychologically. Once you have identified what your soft-spots are, the following techniques will allow you to manage them:

a) Differentiate between your own emotions and the feelings of other people. Know what you are experiencing and what is causing it. This is the key to being able to manage your own thoughts and desires. If you are absorbing negative energy that is affecting you emotionally, step away from the trigger and isolate yourself so that you can process what you are feeling. This is another example of discovering the origin to control the outcome.

b) Set limits and boundaries. Energy vampires, narcissists, and manipulative people are all drawn to empaths because they are naturally compassionate and are, therefore, more prone to people-pleasing. Helping others is part and parcel of having an empathic nature. When you start feeling other people are draining your energy, infecting you with their negativity and treating you like a doormat, it is time to put up boundaries to protect yourself. Being sensitive is not synonymous with weakness. You should always be diligent in safeguarding your interests and ensuring that you are not allowing toxic people to transfer their stresses to you.

c) Surround yourself with positive things. Empaths cannot get away from emotional contagion. Your hypersensitivity means that you will undoubtedly be affected by the feelings and intentions of the people around you. If you surround yourself with happy, positive people, you are likely to feel cheerful too. In the same way, Negative Nancy's will transfer their toxicity and stress to you. Make a conscious decision to surround yourself with things that do not steal your energy, this is what taking charge of your own outcome entails.

d) Alone time to combat sensory overload is a common reality for empaths. Take time off for yourself to limit the intensity and quantity of emotions you have to process. Meditate, affirm your closeness to Mother Nature, or simply sit in a room listening to your favorite music. Enjoying your own company gives you downtime from sensory input and allows you the space to focus inward instead of on other people's emotions.

Step 2: Know Your Gifts

All empaths have natural abilities that stem from their increased emotional awareness. Some of the major empath gifts are:

> Empaths are natural healers and nurtures.

They have limitless energy and are able to offer emotional and physical healing to others using their gifts of nurturing. Some empaths have a natural affinity for animals and can sense what the creature needs. Others are plant empaths who have a natural inclination to love forests, plants, and greenery in general.

➢ Highly intuitive.

Empaths have a well-developed sixth sense that enables them to detect things and intuit what is likely to happen. They are emotionally driven and their mind is very adept in discerning possible danger or imminent occurrences. For instance, some sensitive individuals can sense natural disasters before they happen.

➢ Good at reading people

Empaths can see right through people's emotions and intentions. Their sensitivity to external energy and feelings means that they can easily tell if a person is fake or genuine. This natural ability to read people through body language and non-verbal cues mean that most empaths are emotionally intelligent and have high perception ability.

➢ Creative and innovative.

Empaths feel before they think, meaning that they have a unique way of seeing the world around them. They are especially gifted in arts such as painting, music, and even writing. Those with empathic tendencies can express their emotions creatively, and tap into your natural ability for self-expression through different mediums.

➢ Enthusiasm for life

When an empath feels good, they feel really good. Since they feel emotions so deeply, there are no lukewarm or apathetic approaches to life when it comes to these individuals. They have lust and a zeal for life that's unmatched. Passion beats skill nine out of ten times, so their enthusiasm is great for productivity both professionally and on a personal level.

Step 3: Remember What Is Most Challenging for You

As important as it is to know what your sensitivities are, knowing your triggers is equally vital. Learn what upsets your emotional balance and make a conscious effort to remove it from your life. An empath should realize that their first and most imperative role should be self-love. This will involve avoiding all the triggers that are energetically draining for you.

Energy vampires are toxic individuals that act as vacuums for your happiness and enthusiasm. Their effect on you could be either intentional or accidental, but the end result is the same. These individuals will see lasting damage done to you and your trust. They are concerned with themselves and will eat up the attention and affection that you offer, with nothing to show in return. They are dangerous and unhinged. Imagine a child, complete with infantile selfishness, residing in the body of an adult. Imagine that they care only for what you can do for them. They are narcissists and abusers. They are perpetually sad and miserable friends who appear to be drowning. When you offer your hand, they pull you beneath the crashing waves to save themselves. If you experience any of the below symptoms, you should realize that you are dealing with an energy vampire and cut them off:

- You feel fatigued and inexplicably tired when interacting with this person.

- Suddenly mood shifts from positive to negative when dealing with the individual.

- You feel anxious and uncomfortable in their presence.

- They talk non-stop and don't give you a chance to express yourself.

- They cause you to doubt yourself and your reality. Your opinion of yourself falls drastically when they are near.

There are other triggers for empaths such as boisterous and aggressive behavior, loud noises, limiting or highly structured environments, social gatherings, and many others. Remember that your challenges may be unique to you, so the important thing is identifying what they are and avoiding them. Take note of the instances where you are left feeling drained and uncomfortable.

Step 4: Good Listening and Boundaries

As an empath, our natural compassionate nature makes us want to come to the aid of others and try to fix their problems. This means that sensitive individuals may want to take on other people's responsibilities without giving the person time to come to their own conclusions. This tendency can prevent effective constructive communication and listening skills that incorporate the use of boundaries. You must allow your loved ones to make their own mistakes.

Some good listening strategies include:

➢ Refraining from making suggestions or offering advice.

➢ Do not interrupt the other person.

➢ Use questions to prod and enhance your understanding.

➢ Pay attention to body language.

Step 5: Empowerment

Empowering yourself means leaning on your strengths and abilities and learning how best to utilize your empath powers. Strategies for empowering yourself;

1. Self-awareness – Knowing what your strengths are will give you the ability to lean on them when problems arise. Find out what your own passions are and what you are naturally drawn to. If you are an animal empath, find a way to use your gift by working as a vet or a zookeeper. If you are passionate about helping others, volunteer for charities or get a job with a humanitarian organization. Ultimately you will be much happier doing something that holds meaning for you.

2. Lean into your intuition –As an empath, our greatest

weakness is trying to suppress our emotions and intuition. When you do this, you are negating the power of your gifts. Trust your abilities and your sixth sense to guide you to your destiny. You are the only one who is able to give your life meaning. Playing to your skills is a great way to further your own cause.

3. Rejuvenate and recharge - Emotional steadfastness is essential if you want to remain productive in your life. Balance is necessary for maintaining healthy relationships and allowing you to stay in control of your actions and behavior. Addictive tendencies occur as a result of the failure to manage and process emotions properly. Finding a way to destress and offload excess feelings is important for your psychological well-being.

Some effective strategies for rejuvenating include;

- ❖ Spending time in nature.
- ❖ Meditation.
- ❖ Yoga.
- ❖ Physical exercise.
- ❖ Alone time.
- ❖ Detoxing with water using baths.

Find the method that best suits you and use it as an emotional outlet whenever you feel overwhelmed.

Step 6: Grounding, Clearing, Realizing

Grounding is an effective way to reclaim a sense of balance and reduce sensory overload.

Grounding works by:

- Restoring emotional balance by relieving anxiety.

- Eliminating negative energy and toxic emotions.

- It gives an instant sense of serenity.

- Improving mental and emotional clarity.

- Combats fatigue.

Simple techniques that can be used for grounding and clearing to avoid emotional overload include:

- ❖ Use journaling and write down your emotions to help you in processing them and understanding how you are feeling.

- ❖ Expressing yourself through art such as writing, music or painting is a good way to channel your emotions.

- ❖ Shield yourself from negative energy through visualization or severing ties.

- ❖ Create a safe space for yourself where you can express your emotions freely.

- ❖ Spend time alone.

Step 7: Intuition

Empaths have a very strong intuitive nature that enables them to sense and anticipate things that other people cannot. They have an inner wisdom that is powered by their emotions and communicates to them through intuition. However, when we are preoccupied and overloaded with emotions, we can dull our natural abilities.

Clarity of mind and emotional balance is essential in boosting your empathic intuition and any of the below strategies can be used:

> Listen to your gut. Literally.

  There are neurotransmitters in your gut that connect to your brain, so do not ignore your gut feeling. It is one of the ways your body uses to communicate with you.

> Watch your energy.

  Pay attention to how you feel around others, energy drops or feeling drained can be a sign from your intuition that something is wrong.

> Capture your intuitive flashes.

  Intuition typically manifests in momentary flashes that come and go suddenly. Note them down when they occur and use that as a reminder to follow through.

> Mindful meditation.

  Meditation will improve your mental clarity and make it easier for you to tune into your intuition. Practicing this as often as you can, will help you in keeping your emotions balanced and your mind alert.

Step 8: Identify – Appreciate – Understanding – Awareness   –Action   –   Gratitude

Identify Your Emotions

Self-awareness and understanding how you are feeling at any given point in time is an important tool for empaths. Concentrate on your emotions and try to determine why you are thinking in that way. The following questions will help you self-examine.

- What am I feeling?

- Why am I feeling this way?

- Is this my emotion or am I absorbing someone else's energy?

Appreciate Your Emotions

Once you have identified what you are feeling, it is important to accept and appreciate the sentiment. Do not label emotions as good or bad. All emotions are valid psychological responses to external stimuli. If you are sad, understand that there is something causing that response. If you are happy, there will also be a reason behind that. Understanding your emotions means accepting they are the answer to outside actions, and that you can control them.

Understand the Emotion

Once you know what you are feeling, the next step is identifying why. Every emotion starts with the subjective experience that triggers it. If you can find the why behind your reactions, then you will be halfway to gaining control over them.

Consider these questions when trying to understand your emotion;

- What does this emotion indicate?

- What can I do about it?

- Do I like how I am feeling?

Awareness

Build your self-esteem and strive to always have an awareness that you are capable of dealing with the emotion, regardless of how negative it may seem.

To build your confidence, ask yourself the below:

- Have I experienced this emotion before?

- How did I handle it in the past?

- Have other people been in the same situation?

- What can I learn from them?

Chapter 10

Empath and Manipulation

An Empathic personality describes a person who is hypersensitive. They have a highly emotional nature and an innate ability to sense and feel the emotions of other people. They are also highly intuitive and have a greatly developed sixth sense that enables them to grasp energetic undercurrents and emotions that are below the surface.

Empaths are compassionate and natural-born healers and nurturers.

They have a passion for helping others and alleviating suffering and pain. This is why they are considered to be people pleasers. That said, the power that comes from enhanced intuition and emotional sensitivity can be abused and used to manipulate other people.

An empath has an ability to detect and feel other people's emotions and this gives them a high level of interpersonal intelligence, which can be effectively used as a tool for manipulating other people. While most empaths are loving and caring people, there are those who would not hesitate to abuse their natural aptitudes.

Abusive and manipulative empaths will usually display the following character traits;

They were verbally abused as a child, witnessed it in their own family, or were victimized by a previous partner.

- Low self-esteem.

- Explosive temper and a tendency to overreact.

- Control freaks, i.e., like to have the final say and do not like to be contradicted.

- Try to fix or change people to suit their ideals.

- Possessive and jealous.

- Erratic mood swings such as going from sweet to cruel with no provocation.

- Good at deception and lying.

Empath Techniques Used in Dark Psychology and Manipulation

Forms of Emotional Manipulation

1. Isolation — manipulative empaths will strive to isolate you from other people to make you more dependent on them and, as a result, more susceptible to their words. Beware of people who try to separate you from your friends and family. An abusive person wants to yield maximum influence over you and this is only possible if you do not have other people supporting and advising you. They want to be the center of attention at all times and cannot stand having to share with other people.

   In most cases of emotional and even physical abuse, the first sign that something is wrong is the unwarranted isolation of the victim. If the person was your close friend prior to meeting the manipulator, they would start drawing away from you. They will find excuses not to meet up, always be too busy to talk when you call and generally avoid contact with you. The power of an abusive individual is enhanced by this control and the more alone the victim finds themselves, the more influence the abuser is able to exert on them.

2. Dominance — most manipulative people and abusers are control freaks. They only feel good when they are in charge. They will want to make all your decisions, tell you what to do and what not to do and expect you to comply without questions. Control, for the manipulator, is the ultimate goal of their scheming. They want you to submit to their point of

view.

In extreme cases, the controlling party will go as far as telling their partner when to eat, how to dress and if and when she can leave the house. This dominance works so well because a manipulator is good at undermining the self-esteem and confidence of their victim so that they feel that the abuser knows best and should not be questioned.

3. Intimidation – people who feel the need to assert their authority or get their own way will often resort to intimidation to scare you into submission. Aggression and abusive behavior such as shouting, throwing things, getting in your personal space and actual physical violence are all signs that the other person is using this tactic to scare you into submitting and complying.

   Any relationship that causes you to feel threatened either emotionally or physically is a dysfunctional partnership, and you should remove yourself from it.

   Emotional blackmail is also a tool that manipulators use to intimidate you. For instance, a spouse who is always threatening to leave you if you do not do things their way is using this form of blackmail to control you. Giving in to intimidation from others makes them more likely to keep abusing and manipulating you. Following along with their demands may seem like the path of least resistance, but it sets a dangerous precedent.

4. Humiliation - For any kind of manipulation to work on you, your sense of self-worth needs to be damaged. This means

that the lower your self-esteem is, the easier you will be to control. Abusers know that the more they can make you feel bad about yourself, unworthy, ugly, or stupid, the more likely you are to yield to their dominance.

Manipulative people will humiliate you constantly both in private and public to undermine your self-worth. They have no concern for your feelings and will not hesitate to put you down and shame you. Think of a scenario, where one friend keeps making derisive jokes about their overweight peer. On the surface, they may disguise their comments as silly and harmless, but their sole intention is to hurt and humiliate that person.

There are even parents who will consistently shame their own children in an effort to undermine their sense of self-worth. These children may become reserved and closed up because they are afraid to establish relationships with other people. They could also potentially be training new narcissists, as the birth of disorder is always trauma. No matter how well-meaning or close to us the manipulator may appear to be, they are fully aware of what their criticism is doing to your self-esteem and you should always be wary of "friends" or even partners who have an uncanny ability to make you feel bad about yourself.

People who truly care about you will not make jokes at your expense or put you down in public. Learn to recognize the manipulators in your life who are skilled in using passive-aggressive methods to humiliate and undermine you. These are the most dangerous because usually, you will think they are your friends or only trying to help while in actual sense they are damaging your self-worth.

5. Blame games - A manipulative person will never take responsibility for their actions. Even if you catch them in the act and call them out, they will find ways to shift blame and, in most cases, will try to make you feel guilty by blaming you. This is a manipulation technique known as gaslighting; it serves to make the victim feel as though they are going crazy.

It is common for an abusive person to tell the victim, "if you didn't push me, I would not have hit you, "or "I only cheated because you are emotionally unavailable" and many other deflection techniques. Denial is the fallback plan for any manipulator, even when their actions are obvious and clearly wrong. They will endeavor to twist the truth in such a way that the responsibility and fault lie elsewhere. This controlling technique is very effective in keeping the victim under their thumb because once they believe that everything is their fault, they will work even harder to please the abuser. Empathic manipulators can use their ability to sense your emotions to increase your feelings of guilt and deceive you into feeling sorry for them.

How to Tell if You Are a Manipulative Empath

Empaths have an innate ability to read other people. This skill means that their level of emotional awareness is high enough to enable them to use their understanding of other people's feelings to manipulate and get their way. Our words play a big role in people's lives and knowledge of how to influence and play with people's emotions through language can be used as a means of controlling other people.

So, how do you know if you are a manipulative empath? Most who use their emotional awareness to deceive other people will generally have the following characteristics:

1. You play on other people's fears

    Since you can sense people's concerns and fears, you have a tendency to use this to get them to do what you want. For instance, if you were a manager somewhere and one of your juniors was reluctant to do something unethical, you would use their fear of losing their job to coerce them into action. Or if you want something from your partner, you tend to threaten them that you will leave, and in essence, use their disdain for abandonment to get them to comply. Our worries can motivate us to do anything. We all want to avoid the possibility of facing our own demons. Empaths can use their ingrained knowledge to sift out our concerns. Empathic abusers corral our deepest dreads to be used to steer our actions in their favor.

2. You take advantage of people's moods

    People tend to be more agreeable when they are in a good mood. If you find yourself always asking for favors or trying to get things out of people when you sense they are in a good mood, then you might be a manipulative empath. Our emotions affect our decision-making skills. An ill-intentioned individual will bide their time until the other person is in a cheerful mood and then approach. This method offers the most favorable outcome.

3. You overreact or use negative emotions

We all like getting what we want, but manipulative empaths are good at throwing tantrums and overreacting to situations to get the other person to do what they desire. Do you resort to silent treatment when you are denied something? Do you yell, throw things, or become aggressive physically when you don't get your way? These are classic signs of manipulative empaths.

5. You use the law of reciprocity

Empaths are compassionate in nature and readily do things for others. However, as a manipulative empath, you only do things for people when you want something in return. If you only help people who are in a position to help you back in some way, you are a manipulative empath.

Reciprocity works by creating a sense of obligation in the other person to be good to you because you have done something for them. This is not an evil concept on its own, but if you find yourself constantly using phrases like, "but I did this for you, why can't you help me," or "you owe me one." then, you are a manipulative empath.

4. You lie

   As an empath, you have the gift of being able to understand and feel other people's emotions. This means that you know, on some level, exactly want they want to hear to feel good. If you have no qualms about twisting the truth so that you can please the other person, then you are definitely a manipulative empath. Lying is one of the strongest tools that these individuals use to deceive, influence and control others.

How to Use Empath to Attract and Influence Your Target

The following strategies are effective in gaining influence and control over people using your empath abilities and gifts.

> *Mirroring* – people are drawn to people who are similar to them in one way or another. When you mirror other people's speech body language and emotions, you immediately establish a sense that the two of you are similar and this will make it much easier for you to establish an emotional connection. Observe how the other person talks, the phrases they use, their tone of voice and their body movements. When you start subtly mimicking their actions, they will be subconsciously drawn to you and will be more receptive to your views and thoughts.

> *Love bombing* – as an empath, you have a natural ability to sense people's needs. This means that pleasing the other

person will come easily to you because you already understand what makes them tick. Ultimately everyone likes to feel loved and admired. If you show the other person affection and admiration, on some level, they may start reciprocating the feelings. Go out of your way to show your affection. Make your displays of interest constant and extravagant in such a way that the other person cannot get you out of their mind. In no time, you will have the person completely devoted to you and open to your influence.

➤ *Good listening skills* – paying attention to people is invaluable if you want to effectively manipulate them. It works in two ways. One, you get to know exactly what they want or need and you can then use this information to your advantage. Secondly, people like talking and knowing that someone is actually hearing their words. They will want to spend more time with you because you are genuinely invested in their ideas and you allow them to express themselves.

Work on your listening skills, and use some of the guidelines we covered in the previous chapter. Giving others the feeling that you understand them and that you are receptive to their views will bond them to you in an instant. Their connection to you will make them more susceptible to your influence.

➤ *Fear and relief* – when you understand what people's innermost fears are, you can play on these concerns, using them to paint yourself as their savior or a remedy to their problem. For instance, when dealing with an emotionally insecure person, constantly reassuring them that you will never leave them will ensure that they are dependent upon you and attached to your presence. This is a common manipulation technique that is also used in business and politics. Politicians whip up people's emotions by amplifying their fears and then presenting a solution to "solve" the worry. The same principle applies to advertising campaigns and marketing plans, during which companies can tout their product as the one thing you need to avoid imminent disaster. The crafty may even be able to invent a nonexistent predator or lend more attention to an issue that is only minor in nature. Highlight the problem and then arrive with the cure.

➢ *The halo effect* – it may be superficial, but research has shown that others are instinctively drawn to attractive people on a conscious and subconscious level. The halo effect works by making us attribute positive traits to those who are conventionally beautiful. For example, when you see a handsome person, you are likely to assume that they are kind and understanding even before you get to know them.

Use the halo effect and use your likeability factor to draw people to you. Be mindful of your appearance and grooming and always make sure that you dress appropriately for the occasion. People connect to the outside of you before they know the inside, so always remember that first impressions have a lasting effect.

Conclusion

Thank you for making it through to the end of *Empath*. I hope that you found it to be informative. This book should be able to provide you with all of the tools you need to begin achieving your goals, whatever they may be.

There can be no greater freedom than the ability to be who you are with no reservations. Empaths are given so many unique tools, from birth. These individuals have the ability to greatly better their own lives and the lives of those adjacent to them. It can be difficult to overcome the emotional barriers that come with such abilities but this book aimed to help readers with just that.

It is never too late to learn and get better. Growth is ageless. It doesn't matter how old or young you are, all that matters is that you are committed to exploring your gifts and empowering yourself. The only thing that can truly hold you back from living your best life and making the most of your gifts, is you. When you accept yourself and acknowledge your true nature, everyone else will find it impossible to resist your charms. Confidence and belief in your abilities will take you from being a hesitant empath to a powerhouse.

The gifts you possess as an empath are abilities that you can use to make a difference in the world and touch other people's lives. Ultimately, an empath is a natural healer, nurturer, and protector. These are all qualities that the world sorely needs at this point in time. Let your compassion, creativity, and enthusiasm for life transform you and the people connected to you.

Now that you have enhanced your knowledge of what it means to be an empath, how to use your abilities and manage challenges, the next step is to start practicing the techniques and strategies outlined in this book. Start realizing the gifts that come from your empathic powers. You are the author of your own destiny. Watch yourself transform into the image of the person that you have always wanted to be. Good luck on your journey.

Finally, if you found this book useful in any way, a review on Amazon is always appreciated!

William Cooper

CPSIA information can be obtained
at www.ICGtesting.com
Printed in the USA
BVHW091100220221
600778BV00007B/600

9 781801 794961